POETRY SALZBURG REVIEW

No. 25
Spring 2014

Editors: WOLFGANG GÖRTSCHACHER
ANDREAS SCHACHERMAYR

Editorial Board: ALLY ACKER
WILLIAM BEDFORD
ROBERT DASSANOWSKY
JOHN MATEER
CAITRÍONA O'REILLY

Wolfgang Görtschacher, University of Salzburg,
Department of English and American Studies, Unipark Nonntal,
Erzabt-Klotz-Str. 1, 5020 Salzburg, AUSTRIA

psr@poetrysalzburg.com
www.poetrysalzburg.com/psr
www.facebook.com/poetrysalzburgreview

© Cover design by Andreas Schachermayr

© Cover artwork: "Entfremdung" (2004) by Siegfried Zademack
(http://www.zademack.com/)

Copyright of individual items remains with the contributors.

Only unpublished contributions, including those from literary agents, will be considered. Please add a short bio/bibliographical note. For further details please read our submission guidelines on http://www.poetrysalzburg.com.

ISSN 1561-5871

Printed and bound in Germany by Offset Friedrich, Ubstadt-Weiher
(http://www.druckerei-friedrich.de/)

Current Prices:

	United Kingdom (cash, PayPal, £-cheque)	European Union (cash, PayPal)	USA, rest of the world (Airmail) (cash, PayPal)
Subscription (2 issues)	£ 13.00	€ 15.00	$ 25.00
Students/unwaged/OAPs	£ 11.00	€ 13.00	$ 23.00
Single Copies	£ 7.00	€ 8.00	$ 13.00
Students/unwaged/OAPs	£ 6.00	€ 7.00	$ 12.00

CONTENTS

SMOKESTACK BOOKS

Smokestack Books

is interested in the World as well as
the Word; champions poets who are unconventional,
unfashionable, radical or left-field and working a
long way from the metropolitan centres of cultural
authority; believes that poetry is a part of and not
apart from society; does not think difficulty in poetry
is a virtue; argues that unless poetry belongs to
everyone it is not poetry.

Smokestack poets

include Victor Jara (Chile), Yiannis Ritsos (Greece),
Francis Combes (France), Andras Mezei (Hungary),
Martín Espada (USA), Gustavo Pereira (Venezuela),
Rocco Scotellaro (Italy), Nikola Vaptsarov
(Bulgaria) and John Berger (France).

SMOKESTACK BOOKS
PO Box 408, Middlesbrough TS5 6WA
e-mail: info@smokestack-books.co.uk
tel: 01642 813997
www.smokestack-books.co.uk

SMOKESTACK BOOKS

EDITORIAL

I became a member of *PSR*'s Editorial Board by, of course, being a poet myself. And as any poet, I have my stockpile of rejections, many from magazines that have previously accepted my work. Recently, one such journal wrote back (after the annoyingly requisite five months) about an eleven-line poem I had submitted. The editor liked it, but he didn't care for the second line.

There are many ways to run a journal, as many ways as the editors that create the multitude of little mags that paper our universe. Some editors are mute. If they don't like a poem, they reject it outright without comment. Some editors like to throw bones, and say things like, *Interesting. Try us again*, but reject your work anyway. Some editors feel the writer's word is sacrosanct, and that input from the editor is inappropriate. This particular editor in question said he might or might not accept it, depending upon his take on a different second line.

I have a friend, an excellent poet, who for me echoes the work of Robert Frances, only better. This friend abhors the world of critical editors. He once sent me a batch of new poems, I assumed for my feedback. When I commented on a couple of lines that didn't sit easy with me, he raged, *I know what I'm doing!* This shut down any further communication for a good long while. He rarely sends his work out anymore, ranting that the world of academe has ruined creative writing, and has especially ruined him. *It turns great writers into people who use words like 'pedagogy'*, he says. More often, I suspect, the rejection of his poems feels like someone is criticizing his very soul. So he has taken, what I call, the Salinger approach. He has cut himself off from the world of professional writing. More the loss to the world of literature. I mean this sincerely.

As I suspect is the case with many of us, he is not the only good writer who has gone into hiding. The best poet I ever knew was abused so badly as a child, that the mirror of her drunken mother follows her wherever she goes. She does the job of rejecting her own work before giving the pleasure to any anonymous editor. She's never published a book, and only early in her life did she send out poems for small journal publication. She gifted me a personal ream of her work 25 years ago. It's still one of the favourite reads on my shelf. But I can't tell anyone else to go to a bookshop and buy it. And it makes me sad.

It's vexing when an editor of a magazine rejects your work, especially when they've accepted it before. Back to my earlier story, the editor of said magazine wasn't rejecting my poem. He just wasn't accepting it. He didn't give me clues as to what wasn't working for him. He just implied I should *try something else*. This can be confusing. When you write a poem, you balance all the forces of nature. In the most magic of times, you open up, and you are a conduit for the universe to whisper through you. Whatever emerges doesn't feel has come from 'you' at all. If someone compliments me on a piece that has arisen from one of these magical moments, I honestly don't feel I can take credit. I don't feel 'I' am its author. My body was simply the method used to give it form.

Every artist knows what I'm talking about. So that when I went back to try and revisit the moment of the poem, it was like wandering in a fun house after hours in the dark. I tried, I prodded, I flattered, I nudged. All to no avail. Interested in seeing my poem in print, I *manufactured* a different second line, and sent it off. I was almost relieved when three days later the editor replied, *Nope*. I went back and tried again. This time, I donned my *clever* cap. Surely a smart-ass second line would grab him. I pressed send again. *Nope*.

With this third rejection, I honestly got hopeful about the world. I was so grateful to know there was an editor out there who could smell a fake, and cared enough to play badminton with one small, lone writer. This is a publication that has come out quarterly for the last thirty years, has an enormous readership, and the editor still cares enough about *every word* to dig ditches until he unearths a gem!

I went to sleep. I let it go. So be it, my poem would not be published. Days went by. Weeks. One morning I woke, opened my hands, and the light I carried rose up. There it was. *The line*. It was so simple. And it did not come 'from me'. I don't mean I plagiarized it. I mean I woke, and it had landed on my tongue.

You can't cajole the real thing. You can't flatter it, you can't tease it, and it will not lie down easy for blackmail. You have to get quiet. You have to let it go. When I sent the poem back to the editor with the new line, I knew. *Of course*, he responded. And he took my poem.

Every artist knows these moments are rare. We know that most of what we 'make' is more manufactured *by* us, than comes through us. If we are honest, and unless we are Picasso, only a tiny percentage of our trials unearth as gems. That editor's willingness to hold the space and not recant made me a better writer. I had to work for it, though I couldn't 'make it happen'. I couldn't force it.

Whenever I receive a submission to *PSR*, I don't read it on the computer. I never allow myself to read the bio of the contributor before I read the poems. I want to meet the poems as themselves, without any history mucking up the works. I print the poems out, and they sit until I can get quiet enough to be with them. There are often lines that irk me in a poem I may otherwise like. And like that editor did for me, I would like the luxury to dialogue with the poet, to offer the space, and especially the time, for something else to happen for the poem, so the piece may actualize into its fullest potential. But sadly, unlike that other magazine, *PSR* has less man/woman power, and far less resources. We are deluged by work that pours in from all over the globe. There is simply not the time. There is only the possibility to yea or nay a piece. But I would like writers, and also readers, to know that every word that comes across this desk is always championed first, and evaluated later.

I once received a rejection slip that said, *This almost made it.* What the heck does that mean? I offer this to those of us who have given up putting out our best selves for display. I offer it to that small voice inside all of us saying, *I'm not any good. No one will like it. I don't matter.* Sometimes we need to invoke an invisible circle of our personal champions to remind us that one editor's response to your work is only that – someone else's opinion. It is not <u>THE TRUTH</u>. It has not been uttered as a testament from on high by the Gods.

When my little poem was published, I typed the title of it into Google. It came up on someone's blog who had referenced the poem, and said, *I wish I had written this.* I wish I had too. But how much more meaningful that the universe penned it instead. Take the plunge. Send us your best selves.

Ally Acker

Whistling Sands

The waves rolling to the shore and breaking.
Seeing this through many eyes, the waves
crowding to the beach and turning over, watched
by the generations. Our attention turns and wanders,
preoccupations block transmission: what we do,
the results we have, elsewhere. The land stretching away
behind us, full of snares and recompenses, the angels'
eyes in the cemetery, stone spheres seeing to eternity.

The baby's eyes seek proximity, the sheltering arm,
and any unfamiliarity can be referred to questions of dinner,
but return again and again to the funny thing, whatever it is,
making this noise and repeating itself and spreading
across the sand. The old man's eye is uneasy,
glimpses wandering shades and suspects a darkness
advancing into the corner of his vision, in the distance,
and worries, with little hope now of shifting the structure.

By what mechanism shared senses come together,
and, hearing the salt hit the sand, form an alliance,
which carried through language into act could move
against harm, like forming a household, a mutual trust.
The wild waves weave and the whole land
faces this edge in the arms of a connected script ...
But the child is frightened, and the old man is tired.

Whistle across the sands and there at the far side
of the great sweep of bay is the black ghost itself,
stepping out of the concrete retail shed and coming
towards you, the invited ghost, the relayed failure.
And the baby sees it, and points to it, and laughs.

Immigrant

Driving the long road at night in the rain
rains so hard I can hardly see the road. Looking
for something. Highway 13. Looking for a family,
a contract, a greengage tree heavy with fruit,
a lost child, rain comes down so hard windscreen
can't take the rain, driving through the night, rain
beating on the car's roof. Moving out, heading
for another city, another cheap outskirts, looking for a job.
Rain, rain, never stop. And I remember
walking the thin path through the meadow grass
to visit my sweetheart's house, darkness of
fate descending slowly on me taking steps
in the right direction and the sky could have done anything.

That fine darkness of the soul from which no one needs rescuing.

"At the end of the garden ..."

At the end of the garden behind the shed
with pork pie and birdsong
that was me there on the wooden bench.

The robin perched on my armrest.
The cat forgot it died
and came to curl beside me.

Faint leaves descend the air
turned by a rising warmth, so
recently I was there.

A slight space such as
Helen sought in Egypt,
to return as a wraith.

Four 12-Line Poems

Wilful impoverishment, O evening star.
How will you guide us past that? How
do we meet hands over the hilltops when
both of us are vapour? Your work is to hold
the sky together, mine to hand in a letter of
complaint at the Town Hall, but your reach is
wider, covering the dome from east to west
and thus sang the old man: O Night, O Book,
O star in the water … Listen, there's a man
in the streets of Leeds in the rain in the big
Christmas crowds singing into a microphone,
"take my whole life too".

*

Jeremy Prynne I wish I could play the archlute
to your physical ear. And we would walk together
over the dark moorlands believing in something
I don't know what. Some call, some night music of
stop and start, some tremble between beliefs.
There are many I walk with. I walk with Wordsworth
and with Shakespeare who constantly disappears
and Hardy, guide and spokesman. Sometimes
hundreds of us walk the tired dark page, water
with stars in it leaking into our boots, eradicating belief.
But a crowd worth joining. Not a protest.
A recognition of earth in the moon's clearing.

*

The final recapture of the world, to end on an open fifth
like a forest path ending in a prospect of small towns
distributed across the agricultural plain which seems to say
that all is well enough as far as we know or everything
worth knowing about is under permanent threat. Sometimes at night alone on the open moors every condition
of death surrounds and tramps about me, deaths

of everyone I knew when young auntie this
uncle that no trace but still the face smiling up
at me and fading into the dark hills they never knew
with a wish for a child's success. At the end of this walk maybe
a pub or a bed to rest my head aching with world.

*

Ending at an open space, the whole dome of sky
bonded over us and the star of the sea
washed up on an earthen bank as the question
about poverty and exploitation, shining in the darkness.
Will anyone ever answer? In the winter 12/13
I became, very suddenly, an old man. The voices
on the night moor are stones in a wall, rained on
until the water reaches the footing and
flees to the town. Until society and economy
are brought to support each other, until the trees
fall into the river, until the stones weep, there
are badly swollen people among us.

HARRY CLIFTON

The Month of the Caesars

When summer holds its breath
Before autumn, and the wind dies
On certain days without season
And heaves, on other days,

In the time-rich trees,
And your birth-sign, leonine,
Lights up its constellation
Crowded with shooting-stars

And burnouts, the beginnings
Of clarity and chill – behold yourself,
Small poet, stalled in the provinces,
Chekhovian, going nowhere,

Art nor love, as the Hapsburgs
End their thousand-year empire
In riots, boredom … War,
That will give the lie to everything,

Ripens. Millions will die,
But you, on your old park bench,
Hold nature, history
At bay, for an endless instant.

Above the Clouds

There it is, like breaded snow,
The cloudfield, the deceiving ground
Of existence. Cities, nations
Founder beneath it. Nobody lands.
The plane and its shadow
Fly in tight formation

On a banked white sea
Of immensity. Wedding-flight,
Death-flight, into the eye of the sun,
The muzak-filled ionosphere
Of weightless words, cloud-lexicons,
Hot whiskey and cold beer …

You could rack it up, the balance
Owed to yourself. The price
Of heart failure, burnt-out talent,
Altitude sickness, alcohol highs –
And the music of the spheres
Vibrating in your ears.

Ruins

[...] a thought
Of that late death took all my heart for speech.
                    W. B. Yeats, "In Memory of Major Robert Gregory"

My generation, dropping like flies –
At least in Stalingrad
There were ruins, a battleground.
Here, the buildings rise,
The minds collapse. As John of God
Slides by, a halfway house

For the saint, the suicide
And the family sacrifice,
I stay in lane, in the living tide
Of windscreens and car-bonnets,
Wishing away the silent cries,
The incoming round with my name on it.

The offensive has begun.
A woman walked into the sea
Just yesterday. A man was hung,
Self-hung, from the hook of desertion
There behind suburban curtains,
Disbelieving in victory.

Anne and David, Geraldine –
Enough that I drive by
Once in a while, at the violet hour
Of medication, Gethsemane hour
For the hero, the heroine.
Let me leave you where you lie

Undecorated, even by God,
The children of a neutral state
Who went down fighting, hand to hand,
With your own shadows, self-destroyed,
Caught in the suction of the void
That let the city stand.

Brother

Lo, these many years I have served you, and I never disobeyed your command; yet you never gave me a kid, that I might make merry with my friends. But when this son of yours came, who has devoured your living with harlots, you killed for him the fatted calf!

Parable of the Prodigal Son, Luke 15:29-30

1

I wished he'd stayed, little swine, with the swine.
– I heard the music; then saw my father,
radiant. – Years back, I and he, small brother,
went off playing, got lost; evening came on.

How unfamiliar this track, that stone,
under the indigo sky; kind soother,
I clutched his hand, loved him altogether,
as he trudged, trustful, baby sandals torn –

I would have died for him! Under the high
unhelpful stars we stumbled upon home
at last: out of the dark, the running feet –

our father's voice, calling my brother's name.
Oh, later on he praised me, thanked me:
but that first, panicked cry still kicks the heart.

2

His eyes were sunk far back, his cheeks were thin,
his stalk neck jutted from the gorgeous cloth,
and he was – oddly – quiet; there was a dearth
of joy in him, a rigidness – like pain

beating, but clenched about: both of us, then –
(his crooked vivid way, my decent path)
aged, darkened, melancholy, dull as earth;
treading – it seemed – the pendant years alone.

Our father bustling, full of mirth and tears –
his darling boy! – for me, a pleading smile:
… *always with me, all that is mine is yours.*

Let be, then; let it run, the precious oil,
run down upon the beard. – His belly filled
with husks? – no – no! – dark-traipsing, hopeful child.

Pierrepoint

I conducted each execution with great care and a clear conscience [...] I now [...] have come
to the conclusion that executions solve nothing [...]
                    Albert Pierrepoint (Official Executioner 1931-56)

Nine years' apprenticeship: over and over,
You've got to get it right. – Bentley, marched out
as the clock began to strike: dead

– spinal cord pierced through –
by the eighth chime. – On Tower Hill
the executioners knelt for pardon: drop of balm

in the old hands' clean yerk
of heart to stone. – These random viabilities,
dispersed? – or, only-begotten works, dashed

on the rock of Christ? *It seemed to me*
worse than a thousand murders, Orwell wrote.
How heavy-yoked we are – a strange crop,

saintly, and blind. At horror's eye,
a sudden grace, the kindly scaffold: *Brace up,*
he would tell them, *It will be all right.*

Quotes:
epigraph; l. 2; ll. 14-15: Albert Pierrepoint, *Executioner: Pierrepoint* (1974)
ll. 10-11: George Orwell, *The Road to Wigan Pier* (1937)

Einsatzgruppen

...no longer able to know themselves according to their first condition.

St. Antony of Egypt

They kicked their souls to pulp; drank
to dislocation. Odd, feeble gleams –
some took forbidden snaps: – dark-coated

elders dig; a muzzy queue
stretches off; these three girls, huddled in vests,
try to smile. – Scores of bone-pits,

rustled-over by birch: ... *who blasphemes
against the Holy Spirit*
(old echoes) *will not be forgiven.* Skewered,

clogged with blood, a number
– higher than common – shot their own brains out,
took their darkling chance.

Note:
The Einsatzgruppen ("task forces") were SS murder squads.

MATT HAW

Still-Life in the Orchard

The gardener, idle,
elbow braced against a spade's

handle, reopens some small cut,
smiles away the thought

of turning soil with a little blood.
She's hard to make out, easy

for the many shadows to dismiss.
Perhaps she's made herself a croft,

a house for hiding, where mice
bolt stone lintles before the owl;

the cat kicking his hind legs.
Where all to be heard are barks,

the piddling speech of birds,
the curt greetings of neighbours.

A swallow cuts under the arbour,
to touch the pond's surface

towing distance through cosy bronze.
How much is such. How much is such.

& yet somehow we stand it.
April meets me on the path

to do the little we must do.
The cat refolds herself once & is still.

The Roaring Time

October. The sky's vault doors close.
Atlantic winds scalp bog & burn.
Hinds gossip on the smoke of their breath.

We'll need to coin new words for storm
since it happens all the time. White noise
rain, sculptor's clay clouds,

the angel's share condensed & pangs of loneliness.

The Nip

I think of you gamming
with trawler men. Your recipe
for gull's egg omelette
bartered for a supper of herring
& skein of fishing line.
By nights you are learning
the *Book of Knots* since you've learnt
the tides & ferry times by heart,
can make north without
a compass, your skiff drafting
across the bight where low islands
hang on the horizon like washing
blown to bunch round the line.

Father, send a past life
as you had: petrels & arrowheads
of greylag to mark the seasons;
squally, spitstring rain to simmer
on the sea. Send me wet socks,
a use for the shipping forecast,
a snarl to work bowline & reef.
Turk's head. Clove hitch.

Olivia

Her own shadow's doppelganger
on the kitchen tiles, tilting
her face to acknowledge,
as if for the first time, each
small fuss the world makes:
light insistence of birdsong,
a snapping of wings from the gutter,
flowers mopping pollen on
the window glass.
A sprawl in solitary pride.
An engine of contentment.

*

Whisker still, then tired
of repose – capriciousness
a birthright. What if I
were to match her like
for like? Pour, one moment,
a dish of cream, then next:
fleck her with water, pluck her
mewling by the nape
& set her on the step.
She'd quickstep off as on glass
or flint, ill omen of garden
paths. So quietly. The bramble,
ivy & scutch grass open
a secret door by the fence
& let her in.

Winter Town

Saltiers of wind & sand
kicked through the teeth;
the North Sea casts out
its bath toys here:
a collapsed ball, dreads
of kelp, fossil wood,
a half rotten seal carcass
like a broken draining rack.

To call it home would stick
in the throat, so I abide:
a little bitter & *p'whit*,
a prayer to the grungy gods
of jumper & jackboot;
on one hand the tides
& greetin' terns, on the other,
a row of hare
throwing shadow on the sedge.

[15]

Effet de Crépuscule

An inlet with a bay at the back of its mind puts you in mind
of Cuisin's crepuscular waterways, how they seeped, it's thought,
into Chopin's nocturnes, straight lines of branches and towpaths
and railings as nothing compared with the pleated notes
in which darkness folds and unfolds itself along a seam
of midnight or an edging of backlit cloud. West again,
done with the day, you take the coast road, its tentative bridge
over an away tide. There is a hill you will climb to your B&B
and a sequence of dreams like rented rooms where nothing
is yours but a second-hand suitcase you barely recognize.
You turn. A navy slip of September dusk is pulled down
over upstretched trees and chimneys and telegraph poles.
The town might as well hold its breath the way the inlet does
for the alone woman by a painted tree, barely visible save for
a white headscarf, waiting by a barque that is waiting for her
to step with all her unverbed ghosts out into final light.

Where She Imagines the Want of Being Alone

A small house. Rooms with white door handles
and a dangerous sky to be trapped in window frames.

It is, she thinks, a house for clear glass bowls and
slight intentions. She writes she hears, early nights,

ordinary disappointments rattle, single grains
of rice in a jar, one box inside another.

Something in her wishes to acknowledge
the nothing she has known of love,

but this cannot be the house for that
with its too much time.

Architecture

This wall is my everyday friend
— Le Corbusier

Say what you like
but a five shilling lamp that throws
a hundred dollars at the night

or three nectarines ripening the window sill

makes an offer to a world

that sometimes, I swear,
thinks too much of itself
to accept everything.

Words like stones with sunlight on them
lead me to believe
that if I put what I know into bricks and mortar
and paint the plaster white

or position a square of dark blue glass
underneath a square of red

I would say as much.

The image predicts another image,
one solid phrase and then another
until there is a wall
to depend on

and then a second wall
at a right angle to the first
and a need, suddenly, for a curve

hence the skin of a nectarine
or the weathered edge of stone

or a skim of light
in the vertical evening
that takes on board whys and wherefores

but arrives at the same conclusion
as a morning come dressed in lined grey silk
to take us out of ourselves.

PAUL DURCAN

Near the Sea, Clare Island

After Veronica Bolay

There he is – there you are –
In blue jeans, mustard gansey
At the nets on the sea-wall
Mending them – only
Dying to put to sea
In his death-defying
Skin-currach.

Stooping to his task,
Bent double,
As if digging up
First peat of the year,
Mane of white hair akimbo;
I met him in Roonagh;
He had just died.

Calling up to his fair-haired girl (what a pair!):
"Sure isn't the sea itself also a net
Which I will have to get around to mending?
A turf-rick which one morning I will ferry
To your island home under the mountain cone?
Loaves of turves for your fire-eating feet!"
Akin they laugh the tears of the family!

Sea-Haze (Portnakilly Pier, Clare Island)

After Veronica Bolay

She laps up mist. Why
Does she lap up mist
Insatiably? She
Is in high good form
On days of mist.

"I like mist because
In mist you can
See things

And black currachs on the slip
In mist have
Gunwales of gilt."

The Young Mother on the Country Bus in El Salvador

On a country bus in El Salvador
About twenty-eight years ago
Father Sam found himself seated next
A young Salvadoran mother
Breast-feeding her infant daughter.
Father Sam blurted out:
"*Que hermosa niña!*
What a beautiful baby girl!"
She smiled and when she came
To the end of a passage of breast-feeding
She took Father Sam's right hand
In her own right hand
And placed it across her left breast:
"It is good, Papa" she smiled "it is good."

The Painter Gustave Caillebotte Writing to His Brother, 1877

My dear Martial
Provisionally entitled 'Paris Street; Rainy Day'
It's a choreography, actually, for umbrellas –
Steel-framed umbrellas.
(That melancholy little Belgian maggot Magritte
Years later nicked the idea from me.)
Puzzle is where to pose the umbrellas.
They're all pricked out, of course, unfurled,
So that their pointed tips – eight per brolly –
Constitute a carousel of arousal
Damped down slightly by lightly falling rain,
All our paving stones in heat:
Don't, don't, Marguerite!
Oh do, oh do, Simon!

I posed them on a promenade in Normandy
But changed my mind for I wanted also
To compose an ode to people-watching
In the Place de Dublin
At the intersection of the rue de St. Petersbourg
And the rue de Moscou,
The rue de Bucarest and the rue de Turin.
So I catch in the foreground a couple
Glancing with pointed curiosity
At another couple who are out of picture:
'Is not that Monsieur Simon Lagarde
With the young English lady Mrs Marguerite Fox?
They're both married but not to each other.
A wet day for adultery.'
But it is the can-can of the umbrellas
That is my erotic secret –
More erotic even
Than afternoon tea with my neighbour Bertha!
'Umbrella Can-Can, Paris 1877' –
What say you?
Your affectionate brother, Gustave Caillebotte.

Walking Sequence

1.
A Walk of Mind

Alight from the train at Starcross (holy name!),
follow the empty lane beside Powderham Park
with its Chinese deer and bullrushed stream:
a lane of flowered profusion below one wall
and on the other side a wild silver estuary,
oil-painted tributary of the swaying sea.
Then, thirty minutes or so later, by a church
(brown-red among trees) cross the railway at
a whistle-stop and ascend high-banked path
that ribbons on next the narrowing river-mouth
where herring gulls and herons, oystercatchers
ceaselessly farm salt-griddled, wave-marked crud,
dark mud, forever splicing and un-splicing
seaweed, green, crinkly brown and stone-sieved.
Long philosophical ramble beneath
the cranium of Devon – skies placid or rancid,
both masculine and feminine at once, like Heaven.
And after The Turf Lock Hotel, a white wedge
where waterways meet, estuary and canal,
a liquid Via Appia leading to the city,
lined by reeds and lily pads of summer yellow,
shy mysterious beauty, an aquatic imponderableness
in its mirror-like meandering memory.

Take the walk from Starcross sometime.
Stop by for a drink at the Double Locks pub.
Go on, on through Exeter's slowly gathering suburbs,
to the old port, not much of a port now;
rather the dead end of another time preserved
in this present-future for 'something to see':
a great boat-less basin beneath a cathedral hill.

And though tired by the all of ten miles
you will have tramped, uplifted too you'll find
for that flat long walk is a walk of mind.

2.

There are times – oh yes there are –
when unappreciated you walk so far
it's almost out of life. But, then,
that's self-pity: failing of men
and women. For one reason or another
something leaves you in deeper bother
than life calls for. So don't talk
or complain, but go for a walk
up a dark tree-canopied path
beside a brief stream where waters laugh
and tiny birds, wrens, sparrows
and kingfishers like blue arrows
dart from branch to branch, shadows
of yesterday and so many tomorrows.

It's another walk, loved, that leads
up, up hill, through shadow where light-beads
hang about brown and heavy boughs,
the disabled bush, badger slide to golden brow
of upland meadow set in silent view
against, below, the excited summer blue
of Torbay's sea. A water statement that is
a reflection of mind's many eternities,
very much like what we think and feel
is the real within, yes, the absolute and real.
Shapes of dung-brown branch, or flowers:
oak, apple or blood-bright fuchsia. Amen.

3.

What views? A moon dead white at night.
By day a sun of lemon curd.
Along another lane between mint fields,

bushy banks of piled-up earth,
and the rhythm, the rhythm of body,
flesh and blood that leaks song
and those few vital thoughts:
Is love the possible, the true,
and do we die, full stop, or live
forever? If not, how live at all?
– Soil of the lane is mind-with-stone.
The enigmatic earth we walk upon.

4.

Gender is green. It is also apples, orchards,
harebells feeling the applause of wind, and
the rock-spurt of water from underground.
Let hand caress nature's honeyed land,
stroke the bent, parted grass outwards,
gently rummage each high-climbing mound
that yearns for the kiss of cloud and star.

Gender is green which is the colour of willing.
Circling the fields, tender-bellied to the sun,
where startled larks drop the wayward seed
and hedges are alive with insects' hum,
is to assume one's place in the cycle of making
the flesh-fingering earth of *feeling the need*
for nature's naked uncovering of gender.

Gender is green, a skirt split by distant thighs,
escarpments' musculature of shape and fissure
that is sandstone, chalk, granite and glint.
Everywhere in this domain of need is pressure,
hill-heavy shadow, driving river, flowery gasps;
and when you walk comes the intimate hint
of blood, semen, spirit – nature.

To walk is to celebrate fecundity and drought.
That, in truth, is what walking's all about.

5.

The first stage of the cliff walk is wooded
        feeding glimpses of sea to the sight,
and a well-groomed idyll of golf course is
        unrolled carpetry to one's left.

Elbury Cove affords the first full views
        from its raised beach, stones sea-
licked all along its shovelled-up shore.
        Then a green blanket of turfy downs

sweeps away to Broadsands. Sand, sand, sand
        and seaweed – what children love but
mothers suspect. Then out of this bay
        endlessly rocking, up steep steps

next the steam train viaduct Brunel built
        along a yellow-green path linking place
with views' delight: between valerian pinks,
        white sea campion, the fret of tamarisk

a greater bloom of speckled ocean's glimpsed.
        The cliffs of Roundham Head are livid red.
Paignton's harbour seems an almost private place.
        Boats bob. Folks stare. Geraniums beam.

By then you're half-way to white Torquay.
        Five miles under your belt, and five to go.
With the sea trotting beside you like a dog
        and sun's gold motorboat put-putting above.

6.

It is Foxglove City, a fairy favoured place
I believe in. Into digitalis time. Warfarin,
etc. Many believe the walk (which one?)
is a walk into health. No, I don't believe that.
I believe only in the walk into joy.

On the lane a dead seagull, maggoty.
On the path a worm like an old shoelace.
On the path like black talc, pure dust of summer.
On the path a squashed beetle, black shield.
On the lane hot sun, thermals of joy.

No amount of reality, however nasty,
can prove my – all – life is not joy.
For the Why is: nothing could go on
without that central, intellectually-perplexing
joy – despair's antidote or whatever.

We stride like light into enlightenment. Amen.

7.
On Refusing a Walk

I am here, who refused a walk. Not because
like Coleridge I was drained or sprained
but because I want to contemplate
the meaning of a walk for me. 'Sharp
physical exercise is to be eschewed', said he.
'Why?' I demanded. 'Because it uses up energy,
creative force.' And that I find is true.

So this afternoon, when August limps to September,
I decline to walk. Stay among white flowers kissing green
figgy trees and softly, softly roses yellow bright –
think: so many nameless flowers live and love
in backyard corners such as this …

Let them go, my friends, and walk the tufted hills,
see the Malverns breaking clouds;
a great cathedral humbling a wide plain
and everything from railway silver to racecourse,
fragment of a lake like a shard of withering glass,
and a day of air that drifts through
the calendar of innumerable lives like mine.

The calculation of a walk – such hills – today
is much too much for me. You have
to love a walk or else it's labour all,
an enforced marriage with matted undergrowth,
hard paths, dingy streams polluted
by sheep shit, dirty clay and grotesque frogs.
Walks, as my friend said so long ago,
deplete energy. And like so many things else
justify themselves only if they joy us.
So, once more, it is love we love
a walk for. Love of straightforward going
like into truth.

Painswick Lawn,
Cheltenham 31.8.2002

8.
Jade Green River

Public footpaths. Wooden signs like arms.
Stiles, some stylish, some simply crude,
Walks down dawn-blue lanes, across farms'
alloyed earth, fields cattle-stewed,
noxious, yet in a mostly acceptable way.
And the River Dart's settled presence
a jade-green river through the day
that shrinks with regular tidal absence
then returns foaming to elbow muddy banks
where, either side, the massed trees lean.
River that dominates South Devon, its flanks
threaded with ways to walk and see it gleam.
Parallel stroll to our journey, outer
reflection of inner: a god's walk off water.

9
Sept. 7th Walk

Down a wooded lane soaked in early morning, we discuss man and
nature. At Galmpton Creek a Heritage noticeboard beside a disused

lime kiln recalls the origin of 'white-washing' old stone houses. High-tide in the creek which sparkles in sun as we cross a narrow strand of mud and shingle, pink-shell-strewn, before ascending a long skirt of field to pass through a farmyard where a Baskerville hound rages on a chain. Across the River Dart by ferry at Greenway for coffee on the Dittisham side: a terraced cafe above gently-corrugated waters of light and shadow.

Climb out of Dittisham with its long steep street, its pretty orchard-winding pathways and old muddled houses with over-flowing gardens, to reach a perceptibly-grown East Cornworthy (since our last visit); and after, a panoramic ridge to views of Dartmoor's smoke-blue tors, or Beacon Hill, over Hope's Nose to the south Dorset coast. Then down into the hollow where Cornworthy proper lies:

> There the stranded remains of an old abbey,
> a ponderous stone gateway slap-bang
> in the middle of a field of breathing green:
> haunting ruin of the Middle Ages
> *in media res* of a modern sun-lit day.
> A sweet village curled in its own hollow
> with post-office, village hall and church,
> houses with blackened thatch, their gardens
> full of peonies, geraniums, hollyhocks –
> all the Devon treasury of wilder flora.
> Village blooming with life far from the life
> of cities, with their compressed citizenry
> and competing cacophonies of pointless sound.
> Village with its down-and-up street
> and bird business being transacted
> between tree and thatch, over and under eaves.
> The yellow blister of sun above hills,
> a surrounding web and trickle of light –
> that peace of paradise whose blatant hint
> is everywhere in English summer but felt,
> not seen, like the colours of invisible rainbows.

After Cornworthy we descend, by an overgrown sunken lane, the appropriately named Corkscrew Hill to Tuckenhay near the end of

Bow Creek and, ignoring the famed Maltsters Arms huddled in shadow of the wooded creek, we pass on the short distance to Bow Bridge where the same creek is fed by the Harbourne River. The Watermans Arms there serves soup, bread and honey-roasted ham and many another culinary delight.

Lunch over, more climbs to more views, to eventually join the so-called Dart Valley Trail that winds and curves its way along the west slope of the River Dart to Totnes. In fact, this is a fairly new pastoral foot-and-cycle track. And, it is here, for the first time on this twelve mile walk of ours, we encounter others getting to grips in a like-leisurely fashion with nature. Man, including woman – humanity, that is – constitute the 'mind of nature'. In our walk-talk we have considered every aspect of nature – its mind and body – from Tennyson's 'red in tooth and claw' to the Wordsworthian sublime. And just as we reach the centre of Totnes, about a last hundred yards from the Royal Seven Stars pub, a gentle but sudden shower fell upon us, our talk, our happiness. It seemed nature's own answer: its kind of reason.

KATHRINE SOWERBY

Object Removed

Heavy drapes drawn,
light measured in foot candles,
he protects a yellowing lifespan
from pollution, thieves and silverfish.
All kinds of emergencies at any given time.
His day is limited to mending a moment
on the banks of the River Seine,
the shimmer of light on water.
He prefers night-time, statues
and dark cobbled squares.

Free Fall

What we learn about the life of an inventor
is different from what we come to know – long and unfamiliar.

His whiskers, dampened with water and a wire brush,
his desk covered in apples and oranges, knotted string.

He draws with a mechanical pencil – molten patterns, fields of silver,
lines on linen and model aircraft; synchronised, hand held.

He maps a timber structure and land stretching, stitching
the soil, black and burnt, and runnels of infinite distance.

Is This What Happens at the Point of Impact?

Bed sheets warmed by fire and prisms
of split light. Clouds block the window.
Carved, smoky figures pointing at the glacier;
mottled and streaked like unglazed porcelain.

A Gather

The way honey is picked up,
spooled and viscous. Short puffs of air
at my collar. Perfume and alcohol
lamps and breath – blue bodies
in hot white glass. Hold me
ladle-like – molten and bulky
in our disordered shimmering shop.
Scratch 'chance' into the fruitwood shelves
of tiny blown bottles and blowpipes
that crack and shatter. Your eyes –
green with flecks of copper.
Pick out my detail, glistening
on the polished floor.

Elizabeth Burns

The Field

This summer I've taken to leaving the park by the other gate,
the one further up the road, so I can walk past the part of the field
they've stopped mowing, letting the grasses and the wildflowers
grow so they sway and waver in the breeze; and sometimes
when the weather's dry and the ground isn't flooded and muddy,
I stand here on what once was moorland, looking at the view,
or walk among the buttercups and clover and the sorrel,
the pinks and whites and yellows of the new-made meadow
where grammar school boys from down the hill were brought
to see Catholics disembowelled, the hangings from the gallows.

Because I was in Paris

Because I was in Paris on the day you died,
it's there I want to take you, back to France,
your favourite place, in the moment of your dying.

I want to take you from the darkness
of the crypts below the city, to lift you
carefully, your riddled bones fragile as glass,

and carry you up into the soft October air
where Notre Dame, with its rose windows
and delicate white stonework, soars into the sky

and then I would hold you, weightless,
in my arms, and lay you in a riverboat
and let it take you down the Seine,

pale sun touching with silver the ripples
of the wake and all the yellow leaves falling
and floating beside you on the water.

Grave Goods

Deep bowl, where someone gently placed
twelve hundred years ago these three eggs

and then, perhaps, clasped it with both hands
as if to hold for one last time the body

before it was buried with its cargo of eggs,
bright yolks taken into the darkness of earth

from where, one day, the goods will be excavated,
the bowl chipped, the eggshells slightly cracked.

Your death three weeks ago still raw in me,
I reach out, want to break museum glass,

touch rough pottery and crumbs of earth,
then hold the small eggs in my hand and warm them there.

Invisible

the disease spreading inside her
like a white fern made of frost
on window glass

the god the priest can sense
after the service
in the silence of the vestry

a candle in the daylight
overwhelmed
and waiting for the dark

the soul, you'd think, but he says
it goes in and out like the waves of the sea
he says he can see its colours

CRAIG DOBSON

The Last Emperor

"On 4 September 476 … Romulus Augustulus abdicated imperial office and
retired to the Gulf of Naples with a pension. Historians do not even bother
to recall when he died."

Chris Scarre, *Chronicle of the Roman Emperors*

I picture this last of the Western Emperors:
a figure as diminutive as his name,
haunted at first by fate – the terrible,
unCaesarable indignity of being pensioned off
by his own usurping generalissimo –
but, gradually, acclimatising to his lot.
Maybe he came to feel freed once things
had moved on and forgotten him?
Perhaps he walked the villa's gardens
at evening, watched the burnt umber sun
tumble beyond the edges of the sea
and wondered why he'd ever thought
a famous life worth what obscurity had brought?

Perhaps. Or did it never cease –
his name-failed shame?
Fuelled by centuries of imperial expectation,
did it flower now in constant, bitter reminders –
the sniggering of acquaintances, the disrespect of slaves,
even his own stare refusing the mirror –
so that what he retired to was not
some tranquil compensation or forgiving anonymity,
but a purple cloak of haunting
that no garden stroll could ease,
and a sun forever setting on the world he'd lost,
as he stood in its dying light,
staring out across the darkening waves.

JERZY JARNIEWICZ translated by **David Malcolm**

Straight On

Something grates in the language of love, he thought without words,
when they lay by each other straight on, and his first time
was together when she wasn't in the world. Get it?
Was, but she wasn't. Wasn't, but he was.
How finely the blood pulsed. How a touch outlined,
and the skin learned to speak a text open
as eyes. Sort of the same as today.
Make up time, who knows? he might at this moment think,
and weave those fingers three on three. Time on time.
And the first time. This time turning round,
the trout swam back to the source. They made love going upstream.

A Swedish Cricket on the Hearth*

We got out, but we could have not got out,
the train would have taken us to Świnoujście. And then
a ferry, you know, over the Baltic, to Sweden,
the parish of scan noir.
                              And pornography,
I'd look at in the break in the school toilets.
I still didn't know what it meant in the title, the Swedish word
fucking, and in the color photographs
a dog mounted a woman. *Mounted* – can you say that today
of photographs? Something that seemed unimaginable
was suddenly there to look at and I couldn't sleep. Maybe that's why
I précis for you in bed songs from the late sixties
and in the morning there's a salty swell below.
Salty swell? It's not the Baltic, despite what you'd think.
For that a tongue's necessary. And your taste buds
for a moment in reach.

---

* The title alludes to a 1970s Polish slang term for a pornographic magazine.

A Simple Love Poem

We threw off our clothes
and began to make love so revolutionary
that the seat of the national bank shook,
the stock exchange hit bottom,
and dealers howled from the fire that ate
their bowels and wallets.

We got into each other so utterly that the walls fell
of the overfilled correctional facilities,
and out came avengers with baseball bats and went
to the ministry of internal order.
Police shock-troops scattered,
abandoning shields, helmets and notebooks,
all that was left was a black polonaise.

You mounted me so defiantly that investors
began in panic to pack their bags
and went back home on cut-price planes,
carrying off slapdash Sasnal canvasses,
all they got from their Vistula mission
(a ten-fold rise in price
in just five years).

I swallowed you up like an anarchist, until in ruins lay
the gothic galleries of Tesco and Carrefour,
into the walls melted the armoured ATMs,
PKO BP, Pekao SA,
Lukas Bank, Citibank, Amerbank,
Millennium, Bank Silesia, WBK, Alior,
Inteligo, Deutsche Bank, BPH,
Multi Bank, Fortis Bank, ING and Post Bank,
and a gust of fire blew right through
the crooked corridors of the insurance companies.

I love you. Our naked bodies haunt Europe
like an unfledged unguilty communism.

Catalogue

She, you hear, doesn't hear. Listens –
on her head headphones.
Of signs not a trace, only things remain,
unbearably connected to dumb singularity:
pen drive, mobile, hairdryer with diffuser.
A tawdry catalogue, a prosthesis of order.

She, you see, doesn't see. Looks –
at the fast landscape unfolding out the window:
post-Soviet tank, viaduct, Skierniewice cemetery.
He could take her by the hand, but by taking –
he knows, for how could it! – he'll fix nothing. Not
stop the train. He could reach for traces.
Efface the spoor. Tear off the funereal t-shirt.

Really: it was at her place? On a trip?
In someone else's mirror? In the props room,
laptop, lip gloss, nail clippers,
and not a sign behind? Loses
coordinates. It will not come,
the sentence, or come together on his tongue. Doesn't hear.

Soft Underbelly

It passed, that hot time of velveteen and bug-nets.
The dictionary poorer by a few hundred words
contained despite everything everything.
Well okay, to the first space
after the comma, but right after that
stretched white as a sheet
the stains of high Spitzbergen. To this day
I don't understand why you shifted so diametrically,
and your lips grabbed the attention of the Gen. Sec. of Glaciology,
who to orangeade preferred Paracetamol. I don't know.
Encores – *nie budiet*. We could've been like the gods
of sentences crisp and complex, but there remained for us only
byegone words, *blood, sweat and tears*,
with every winter paler.

Les Enfants terribles: Victor Hugo and Aimé Césaire

Victor Hugo. *How to Be a Grandfather*. Introd. and transl. Timothy Adès. London: Hearing Eye, 2012. 184 pp. ISBN 978-1-905082-66-7, £12.00 pb.

Aimé Césaire. *Notebook of a Return to the Native Land*. Bilingual edition. Transl. and ed. A. James Arnold and Clayton Eshleman. Middletown, CT: Wesleyan UP, 2013. 73 pp. ISBN 978-0-8195-7370-4, US$24.95 hb.

In a cycle of sixty-eight poems, *L'Art d'être Grand-Père* (1877), translated by Timothy Adès as *How to Be a Grandfather*, the French literary giant Victor Hugo (1802-1885) celebrates the perfection of childhood, the beauty and vulnerability of its innocence, as well as his love for children. We see a tender, and more private, side of Hugo who dotes on his grandchildren, Georges and Jeanne. Since the pre-mature death of their father, Charles Hugo, and their mother, the children were entrusted to the care of their grandfather. "A child makes me a stupid ass: / In George and Jean I have a brace. / One is my guide and one my star. / I run to where their voices are; / Jean is ten months and George is two, / Divinely gauche in all they do" (16), Hugo writes with candor in the first section about his "contented exile" in Guernsey.

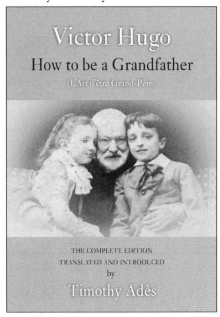

Divided into eighteen sections, this book of hymns contains reflections on happiness, youth, nature, and life, interspersed with meditations on the poet's own frailing mortality. There is humor in several of them, some more entertaining than one might expect. Each section title does the work of overall image and narration with efficiency, indulgence, and poetic intelligence: "Jean Asleep", "Poem of the Zoo", "Old Age and Youth Together", "Grandpa's Childhood Frolics", "Children, Birds and Flowers", "Stones Thrown at Jean", "Epic Story of the Lion", "To Souls Flown Away", "What They Will Read Later On", and so forth. The zoo, in particular, is a subject of great interest to Hugo. In a sequence of ten poems, the Romantic poet praises Buffon, listens to "animals talk" with the curiosity of a child, and muses in "Children and Animals" with a political slant, "What grown-ups think, perhaps the young discover: / A king in his cave, a tiger in his Louvre: / Such pleasure. 'Nice and ugly! Come and see.'" (48)

Although Adès has offered few insights on his strategies and engagement with the work as a translator, I appreciate the brevity of his preface, its light touch a modesty that allows us to immerse ourselves in the Hugolian light verses right away. On the impossibility of translating *alexandrins*, he makes a quick remark: "Translating with rhyme, if done well, is a very demanding labour of love: I had done as much as I could." (6) To conclude the volume, Adès also includes other poems by Hugo: "The Expiation: Waterloo, Moscow, St. Helena", "June 1871", "Good Advice to Lovers", and "Boaz Asleep".

For its new edition published by Wesleyan University Press, American translators A. James Arnold and Clayton Eshleman bring alive in the English language the original 1939 version of Aimé Césaire's well-known *Cahier d'un retour au pays natal* (*Notebook of a Return to the Native Land*). "Our intention in offering the 1939 French text of the 'Notebook', translated for the first time into English", Arnold specifies from the outset, "is to strip away decades of re-writing that introduced an ideological purpose absent from the original." (xx) Composed in a series of prose fragments and free verse, this epic

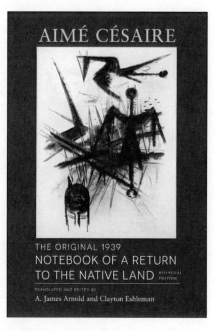

AIMÉ CÉSAIRE

THE ORIGINAL 1939
NOTEBOOK OF A RETURN
TO THE NATIVE LAND BILINGUAL EDITION

TRANSLATED AND EDITED BY
A. James Arnold and Clayton Eshleman

poem, an extended lyrical narrative – to be precise, a "palimpsest", as Arnold has noted in his introductory essay – marked the start of Martinican poet, playwright, and politician Aimé Césaire's (1913-2008) life-long crusade for the *négritude* movement. Dense in its allusions and complex in structure or diction, the work earns its place as one of the most important literary writings of our twentieth century – both in its cultural contexts and linguistic innovations.

For scholars and informed readers, this edition offers fresh possibilities of interpretation for this document and its history as an anti-colonialist manifesto, an anthem of sorts, and a representative topology of the collective colonial black consciousness of that time. In his struggle with racial identity or conditioning, Césaire insists on the viscereal: he capitalizes on the French usage of more qualificative adjectives than verbs, and offers very physical descriptions of the black resistance:

> At the end of first light, the famished morne and no one knows better than this bastard morne why the suicide choked with a little help from his hypoglossal jamming his tongue backward to swallow it; why a woman seems to float belly up on the Capot River (her chiaroscuro body submissively organized at the command of her navel) but she is only a bundle of sonorous water. (7)

and thirty-eight strophes later:

> My heroism, what a farce!
> This town fits me to a t.
> And my soul is prostrate. Prostrate like this town in its refuse and mud.
> This town, my face of mud.
> The baptismal water dries on my forehead.
> For my face I demand the vivid homage of spit! …
> So, being what we are, ours the warrior thrust, the triumphant knee,
>   the well-plowed plains of the future!
> Look, I'd rather admit to uninhibited ravings, my heart in my brain
>   like a drunken knee. (31)

It is difficult to read the work for its aesthetics without any foreground knowledge of its social politics, and even more so to understand or see the heroic – yet anti-romantic – narrator without the lenses from 1939. "How it was meant to be read in 1939" (xx), and to read it as its first audience: this is the task that the translators, both specialists of Césaire's literature, have defined for themselves when they decided to

[38]

dedicate themselves anew to this project. For this reason, it seems natural that choices of translation for Césaire's time-specific lexicon calls for more research and an intuited reasoning. Take for instance, the concluding lines:

> I follow you who are imprinted on my ancestral white cornea
> Rise sky licker
> And the great black hole where a moon ago I wanted to drown
> It is there I will now fish
> the malevolent tongue of the night in its still verticity! (57)

The last word "verticity" warrants visual and sonic attention, even scholarship: *verrition, verri, verrare* ... in short, it is an original translation of a *mot rare* created by Césaire. (Other "Césaireian" words include *morne, un patyura ombrageux, le tracking, le Lindy-hop* ... the list goes on.) If translation must come to terms with notions of strangeness, these words demand an inner listening from the translators, and extra efforts to keep their strangeness, their idiosyncrasy, authentic and unquestioned in their "unstrange" target language. To conclude, I would like to quote co-translator Clayton Eshleman's own poem, "For Aimé Césaire", as an insider's response – a commentary in metaphors – to this poetry he has helped, since the eighties, to "transplant" and be "made fresh" in another language:

> Spend language, then, as the nouveaux riches spend money
> invest the air with breath newly gained each moment
> hoard only in the poem, be the reader-miser, a new kind of snake
> coiled in the coin-flown beggar palm, be political, give it all away
> one's merkin, be naked to the Africa of the image mine in which
> biology is a tug-of-war with deboned language in a tug-of-war with
> Auschwitz in a tug-of-war with the immense demand now to meet the
> > complex
> actual day across the face of which Idi Amin is raining –
> the poem cannot wipe off the blood
> but blood cannot wipe out the poem
> black caterpillar
> in its mourning leaves, in cortege through the trunk of the highway of
> history in a hug-of-war with our inclusion in
> the shrapnel-elite garden of Eden.
> > ("At the Locks of the Void", *Companion Spider: Essays*.
> > Middletown, CT: Wesleyan UP, 2002, 139.)

Get Well Soon!

I guess we're all struggling in some way,
wondering what colour the bus is,
getting to know if the terminus is always where it started.
Once I lived by the sea, on an island.
It never seized to amaze how
the windsurfer skimmed the surface,
whether the waves were broken by boats,
if boats themselves generated waves.
I'd long for rough seas to untie knotted nets
and defy Mediterranean calm.
And the ambivalence of snow …
neither liquid nor solid, earth nor water.
We could die on dangerous roads
deceived by the mountain's enchanting surface
or just get stuck in a drift:
so close to death yet so near to survival.

Barb

Each time your going
is like a sharp tip –
it's lodged,
       it's acute,
              it smarts.

Distance brings parallel stories: while
thinking of spearing cuttlefish
by perpetual light,
I hear you tell of sheatfish
arrowed at night.

We're apart now.

I picture palms clearly:
they're black, made slippery
with sea and squid ink.
Searching for fresh water,
I perceive hooks in the lips
of captured catfish and
wait for your return
to discard the barb.

All this talk of fish and flesh
gives flight to my conviction:
only you can string the bow.

Music Field
Jim Maguire

Music Field
Jim Maguire

Poetry Salzburg

"This is a wonderful collection of poems by a subtle genius who deserves a very wide audience. It is the atmosphere of music, with its structures and disciplines, that both saturates and refines the poetry of Jim Maguire. Language is his keyboard now, and he makes highly disciplined poetry with its inky black keys. His company is Mussorgsky, Brahms and Schubert as he moves through the rooms of life, wondering why the days can turn out for the worst or why it is not enough to merely sit and contemplate. His masterpieces here, 'Duparc: A Programme Note' and 'Before Music' are two of the most perfect poems I've read in many years, but they are only two of at least a dozen astonishing creations. Here is a master who knows the music of what happens, who understands the aliveness of the ordinary. Maguire is the Glenn Gould of our Irish poetry, walking out with 'the purple love / I harbour for the things I fear'."

Thomas McCarthy

July 2013. 72 pp. ISBN 978-3-901993-40-4
£9.50 (+ 2.00 p&p), €12.00 (+ 2.50 p&p), US$16.00 (+ 3.00 p&p)

Rembrandt's *The Blinding of Samson*, 1636

At the gap in the canvas, she turns to gloat,
to take deep pleasure in Samson's capture,
his chaining in darkness, his blinding.
Her left hand grasps the plume of his shorn hair
hanging from her forearm like a shield.
Her right grips shears heavy as a Hittite sword.
But a spasm of fear claws her joyful face:
what if the hero, writhing, should break free
of the dark iron coils and pointed weaponry?
His eyes are clamped shut against the sight
of betrayal. The blade, naked, is her touch.
Taken in a desert dream where vision
was her unruly curls and white body,
he was blind long before the piercing.

Rembrandt's *Bathsheba*, 1654

You are the voyeur. You cannot turn
away. Like David you watch and want.
The old slave scours Bathsheba's feet.
That hag keeps her hard eyes fixed on the task
of making flesh wholly pure – until
the body gleams like a calf bred for the knife.
What is laid bare before you? Uriah's wife
clutches in a fair hand another's letter.
Come closer. Look. Can you read the King's mad script
scrawled on the crumpled sheet? Is it
a death warrant or a private psalm of love?
Intimated on that white gloss – a scarlet blotch,
that wax seal ruddy as her husband's blood,
as woman's shame, as the stillborn child.

Gustav Klimt's *The Kiss*, 1908

These lovers, armored
in radiance, embrace,
shedding chainmail
of platinum and petals.
Heavy his brash head
and bold hands,
her soft limbs
and tilted head
lit pure.
They kneel
in a brazen bed
of rare blooms
rooted in slag.
This kiss, molten,
presses down
to burn off
all the finery
threaded with silver
and all the flowers
perfumed with gold,
the mesmerizing tapestry,
the hypnotic mosaic,
and the garden of the blind.
This kiss craves
the alchemy of one.
It resists
the vast glitz
of old Midas,
his bright cold clutch.

Franz Marc's *Wild Pigs*, 1913

Blue boar
lunging tusks
surly red eye

roots and grubs
through absinthe
tint of foliage

and sulphur
caul of bloom,
unsated

as the whirlpool
of undergrowth
churns and spins.

Behind him roils
in blurred ochre
the Ur-pig.

Below him brims
and flows
the wild sow.

Lured here
to wallow
in oil

these beasts
thud and roil
in muck,

possessed by
the hot stink
of paint.

The Epistle of Martianus Hostilius

I

I want to be the person I am today.
I have just written a very long letter.
I must be very sick.
I am of the sick whom one can count on
And believe when I say
That I have written in one afternoon
About the duration of death
That I have spent a life in lengthening.

II

It was afternoon when this ragged shirt of skin,
That had once been a soldier
Was slit through by this Silures sword.
Late that evening,
With the snow on the ground
All rust-smelling
And soft with my blood,
And the fire a cold, yellow fever
On my lidless eyes,
Our surgeon, Gaius Picus,
Pecked at my torn left arm
And sewed it back
Swearing that the legend of Osiris
Would have been different
Had he been around.

III

Somewhere in the gloom of my burst pod of flesh
My Roman courage had spilled out.
It must be staining
Some cornice of Y Gaer,

Darker than the stone,
Lighter than the day
That feels like a tombstone
At the Sun's burial.

IV

And ever since
The right arm shakes
And snatches
Like I was attempting to write
In a nightmare.
And so I have written this afternoon
When I can feel change
As a torpor whose past
I cannot imagine,
Whose future I cannot see
Over this dark green valley
Of Usk.

V

I wrote to my wife
In her orange-scented villa
Where the walls are white
And the breeze warm
Even in winter
Because, I hear my daughter
Singing to her doll
An Euboean song
Her mother sang to me
When I was home
And bathed, and smelt
Of holly and not of barbarian guts,
Ate olives and played
Hercules and Atlas with my cousins
In a garden where I had
Grown taller than the bushes
Of columbine.

VI

I wrote to my wife:
I asked her if her sibylline song
Had any stanza
About blue lips and white knuckles,
Unyielding scabbards
And crimson icicles of blood
In our fort of fear,
In this dear, alien Cymru.

VII

I have written to my wife:
"Who am I for you after so many years?" –
"A phantom", I wrote
And added twelve blank sheets
Before I signed my name:
Enough space for the bald snow,
The bare un-uddered earth
Here,
Not motherly like the Tiber fields
Beside a strict Rome.
Phantoms are made as well here
As in Rome,
Thus.

VIII

Martianus Hostilius,
I want to walk after you
When you are dead,
Ex epistulae;
Turn around and trace
The turn of the road
From Sarn Helen to the Capitol,
Trace the vines and the moss in the Underworld
Of the Sun's tenure.

(The Usk Valley, December C. 73AD)

Bat Medicine

A tiny bat
Shiny eyes
Fragile
Folded wings
Whispered in
The secret shadows

She neither bird
Nor animal
Neither of the sky
Nor of the earth
But a between-worlds being
Sacred to the Osage

The furred not
Feathered one
Spoke succinctly

Her wisdom
You must grow
To escape
Being swallowed
By the mammoth
Of your grief
You must be
Bigger than what
Will devour you

Only then can
You fly

Hortense and the Burden of Pretense

She was painfully aware of her
Kangaroo heritage at all times.
She tried to hide her
Tendency to hop …
With a fake limp
And long skirts.

She struggled to be dainty with
Her teacup so no one could tell
She was not English
Like everyone else.

With social refinement,
She kept up her correspondence
With her peers even though
The envelopes mixed with her cud when
She moistened them with her
Delicate black tongue.

She was excruciatingly self-conscious
Because her nose was too shiny.
She was certain it was bourgeois
To powder it excessively in public.

She felt that her lumpen ears were too big
Under her fashionable wig. She feared
People would think her a changeling.
She did not wish to appear to be
What she was not.

Her greatest desire was
To give up the pretense of royalty.

Cochiti Pueblo, New Mexico, 1999

Two hundred dancers at Cochiti
Swaying, swinging evergreen branches
Ten singers calling the ancient chants
Children dancing with parents
The women, one shoulder bare
Fawn colored dresses all, tablitas
Long, straight black hair moving, alive
The men, bare chests, western shirts
Concentrating ... focusing.
White observers unsure of the century.

Singers, dancers calling the spirits
For rain, the connection between men and nature
Subtle, gentle communication
Brings rain without domination
But in spiritual partnership

Five years ago no one came
To the compelling dances
Now the plaza is filled with
Those serious, dedicated
A turning, a return of the people
Their tradition, their beliefs.

Intangible

Like ants
Unwelcomed children
Carry away crumbs
Of their mothers'
Silenced selves.

Medication

Does it matter if it is the medication
that keeps him happy,
hyper, sometimes high as the clouds
scudding the sky
where he is a god
in his own distorted mirror,
where birds trill like flutes,
oboes, piccolos,
and sing their paeans in a burst
of mingled sound?

The alternative is to trench
snake-like and scrutting
in the crumbling earth,
where, like Macbeth, scorpions
scuttle around his brain,
where oblivion closes in like a mist
and threnodies are sung.

The medication takes him
up spiral staircases of space
to an errant jubilation.

Feathers
After Emily Brontë

She tears at her pillows and cushions,
the down flying
like snow in a shaken glass globe.

She extracts feathers,
identifying the birds to which they belonged:
turkey, wild duck, pigeon, moorcock.

Then she recognises the lapwing's feathers
and, panic-stricken,
clutches handfuls
looking for red, for blood.

GAIL DENDY

Incomplete

The cat brings in lizards without their tails,
a half-eaten cricket, a rain spider's legs,
and parts of a mynah (the gruesome bits).
It seems nature's denuded,

or at least our back yard.
Hunting's instinctive to cats,
I explain to my kids,

*anything that moves, that's
smaller than him, he'll go for.*
Wendy's eyes grow round,
like the dark universe expanding.
She's smaller than me

and, I sense, beginning to worry.
It was meant to be, I explain. *A sacrifice.
The mynah didn't feel a thing.*

And there I've lied again,
confused the issue. She will
mother me, one day, lie to me

and say I'm looking lovely,
my heartbeat's stable,
my blood count's pretty good,
and leave out the gruesome bits,
the ones that really count.

Devotion is a sort of carnage, really,
like today's haul stacked up under the stairs,
and, with all this summer heat,
beginning to rot.
Love you lots, I say to the kids

in the moments before I drop them off
to spend the weekend with their father.
Before I can finish they're talking to him
about the bird.

It's only later that I boil up a cup of tea,
bundle the wash into the machine,
clean up the entrails and the blood
(making sure to get at all the gruesome bits),
darken the room,
and complete the story.

Salmon Run

My father did not go gentle into that good night,
but like a mottled and speckled salmon, gulped the river
leading from the exhaust through a virgin, plastic hose

and then upstream, it seemed, into the car. For two weeks
we declined to have it cleaned, what with the thought
of that bluish, sweetish cloud having become his shroud.

Of course there was blame, the family splitting like a pomegranate
right before the funeral. I always wondered whether it was
prescience, or misery, or mercy that drove him to it, drove him

statically but deliberately, his hand grasping the wheel
until the very last, his life (and my mother's too) disintegrating
into the blank-walled structure of the garage, the engine
humming like a heart all day, they said, but not too far into the night.

Asking

For Elainie Lillios

I would never capitulate, even for you;
Even more so, especially not for you.

There is such an ever present Eros
And spirituality in the alchemy between us.

So, no capitulation, just because I might
Want to actually please you.

The work of music and words was done
With respect to itself, and my attempt

In creating within a collaboration, which
Is probably one of the most difficult

Challenges, and possible achievements,
To accomplish. I appreciate what you

Did with what I provided you with.
I think the lines regarding the moonlight

And the dusting of snow did deserve to be
Cut. How you arranged the sequence,

Seasonally, from what I provided,
Is a testament to your working with me,

And I with you. Also, I believe I opened
The door for you to *ask for it all.*

It is salient, when a woman does that,
And, as a man, one can stand fast,

In accommodating her request, and he
Pleases her. *Asking for it all* is significant,

Only because the woman who asks for it
Trusts enough to, as you do, with grace.

The Dante Alighieri Summer *Paradiso al Fresco*

It is not yet your vacation, but it could be –
The day being so perfectly lit beneath

The high cerulean sky, dotted with cumulus;
The air so fresh after days of June rain.

You decide to take out the leftover spinach
Pasta and white clam sauce from the refrigerator;

Dust it generously with *Parmesan, Romano & Asiago*,
Rotate several full turns of black pepper

From the wooden grinder, and drizzle a couple
Of tablespoons of virgin olive oil over all of that.

You have worked your way through all the levels
Of hell: the job, your boss, an irascible partner,

And then persevered through all seven
Of the purgatorial circles, much described

By that beloved flirt, Saint Theresa of Avila,
Who it is said levitated several times in the galley

Kitchen of the nunnery to the extent that
Her fellow sisters needed to pull her by her habit

Back down to the ground. By now you can use
A respite in paradise, although a half hour would

[55]

Do; besides, where you find yourself now
Appears to be the Florian, a sidewalk café, with

The most fascinating of angelic faces at each table.
In your abandon, you order the side salad to go

With the pasta, which is simply called the *Al Fresco*,
Combining chick peas, cucumber, and Vidalia onion

In blue-cheese dressing. When the waitress
Takes your order, you don't notice the size

Of her wings until she turns to go; and before
You can speak the thought, she turns back around

And suggests a drink that she believes best to
Accompany your meal. As you take another sip

Of the iced cherry juice with orange seltzer,
You notice the trio sitting at the table next to you.

Proffering his violin as the sacred object that it is,
Is Vivaldi; then beside him, Dante is sharing

Photographs of himself and Beatrice, taken
On their vacation in the Pyrenees, to Botticelli,

Who is sitting in front of a plate full of empty
Shells from his abundant appetizer of clams casino –

All three originals beaming in the verisimilitude
Of their specific and inimitable perfections,

All seated beneath a sword of light the Archangel
Gabriel is holding above them like a torch of flame.

IAN C. SMITH

The Secret Sound

The maddeningly familiar sound was played,
with advance warnings, at intervals on the radio.
Mother loved to guess the amplified recording.
She'd scissor entry forms from *Women's Weekly*,
or was it *Palmolive* soap wrappers, or *Lifebuoy*?
collecting as many as she could afford.
The prize was large, in pounds back then,
and our family always seemed to need
more than our nightwatchman father earned.
These scissors, or a chair, a plate, an iron,
were hurled with eerie moans at him or us
from a maelstrom of harboured rages, rages
similar to those of her crazy ex-army father.
She also bought lottery tickets.

One bonanza was a luxury Gold Coast house.
She planned to gather us behind the palisades
of this Taj Mahal of multiple en-suite bedrooms
where we'd live the life, or lives, of Riley.
When we were grown her kids had escaped
into the dubious refuge of first marriages.
Sons- and daughters-in-law lived their way,
didn't like her much, or get along,
might not expose their own children, despite greed.
Mother's Kennedy-style compound idea left out
the incomes we'd need to cavort in those bedrooms,
perhaps from jobs landing in our sun-blessed laps;
and that we might say no to her dream
about winning before it grew too late.

Aqueduct Days

The shack, of course, has gone for good;
the donkey I rode, showing off, toes skimming grass
as kookaburras derided my laid back style,
even their tall eucalyptus trees, gone too.
I remember her lying belly-down over me
at right angles so we formed a cross.
I gazed up, blood throbbing in delirious swoon,
at sunlight filtered by a pentecost of tree-ferns,
the day's tingling ache reaching towards dusk.
She was my nature girl that blessed summer
of our moist exchanges in the dappled light;
a daisy chain encircling an ankle,
a charm bracelet tinkling from her wrist.
Her smooth body now seems an act of grace,
naked perfection seen once then never again,
our walks along the aqueduct ridge
past the coolness of those moss-packed slopes
the place to which I would go back
if granted just one time travel voucher
but no voice returns, not mine, nor hers
though I'm speaking her name.

Contender

For Joe

Almost September, winter's end, alone by choice,
hooked on a film, muttering, hands like birds.
My familiar docks' rusty halls; a foraging dog
prowls the remains of fire on stained concrete.
I breathe coal dust, break bylaws but blend in.
This is the 'fifties of my strange boyhood,
the Port of Melbourne's brick and iron bowels.
A barge hoots near Constitution Dock's dark sheds.
Place intertwines with happiness.
This entrepôt is my mise-en-scène.

Near a goods embankment I reprise *Waterfront*,
the Yarra the East River's stand-in.
Pigeons rise from a broken sawtooth roof,
clattering through mist over oily water
as I flip Terry's collar, the air chill and damp,
quick fists burrowing in jacket pockets,
keeping a hopeful eye for an angel
with Edie's face, convent-innocent, unlike mine,
who might understand, even share,
my dream of making the big time.

COLIN PINK

Another Day, Another Pawn Ticket

How the words bubble up, a logorrhoea,
like the frantic song of the skylarks,
out of control, spilling from the mouth,
tumbling together, heedless of art.

Such ecstatic music the Maenad's chanted,
words to tear us limb from limb. We yield
but always stumble from the wreckage
then hitch a lift to another battlefield.

Miles Davis blows a smoky melody,
his trumpet becomes as soft and pliant
as a lover's lips wed to his for this brief
abandonment of original silence.

Some words are strong, some are weak,
yet bruises blossom beneath their touch.
Map-less, without direction, I ask myself
how we could have forgotten so much.

Pick up these moments, scattered pennies,
I want to place in the jar of memory

saved for some future time, a down-
payment on a long sought harmony.

Tear off another page from the calendar;
each leaf becomes, it would seem,
a pawn ticket to another moment
I'll never have the wealth to redeem.

Victorian Woman in a Green Dress

After a painting by Vittorio Matteo Corcos, 1896

You look out defiantly as if to say, What
do you have for me? Impress me, go on.
You are waiting but your thoughts are elsewhere;

they drift free, like the loose strands of hair,
thought tendrils, that curl about your head.
What are you looking for, here on the bench?

Your eyes are not saying, nor your lips, as your
chin rests on the soft plinth of your hand, fingers
gloved in a second skin of supple leather.

Beside you the pile of books, in soft yellow covers,
suggest a taste for the decadent, the frisson of
forbidden literature and heat between the sheets.

This rendezvous was arranged long ago
and now we have forgotten why we came.
I am late and everything has time's patina upon it.

The leaves are etched with so many mottled
memories. And now I see the sorrow in your eyes.
Are you alive or an illusion of someone from long ago?

The leaves fall and petals wilt; the warmth of the day
retreats, chill night returns. Let's unwrap time, peel
back each brittle layer, until we might meet.

Sea Time

We're rigged with history, regardless of GPS and weather faxes,
goosing closer to *The Endeavour* than *The Enterprise.*

Despite hours being regimented into columns
for the log, highs can vaporise
above the cumulus at the sea's rim.

Still, an internal alarm alerts me
to the forecast: 0730, 1930.
To keep up
I score chords to the coastguard's refrain.

The tidal atlas flows with the set and drift
– six hours after high water – six hours before –
for today, tomorrow, next week, year and decade
in the riffle of twelve pages. The same twelve, over and over.

I become mesmerised by the endless prediction, hammocked
in this flickbook of assurance.

A quick piss overboard trickles into phosphorescence,
and the 42 mph of a distant gale creeps closer
fingering up each vertebrae of lives lost.

On a stormbound anchor gravity zig-zags,
standing still is acrobatic.

With a stab at progress, head to wind,
everything blows apart,
our cheeks whip hollow, ears howl,
sails gurn.

On the helm, my focus needs to be fleet:
bearing, sail, depth; bearing, sail, depth.

Counting seconds between the lighthouse flash,
measuring those deep unsounding holes of night,
calls for the grease of stars,

the drawl of longitude.

Overwintering

Stripped to its hull,
without sails, ropes, without bunks and electronics,
the boat runs with condensation.

Rigged and rolling
it mythologizes whoever's on board.
Odysseus, Columbus, Crowhurst
all throw their shadows

over even the shortest passage.
And if the sun's behind,

I cast my own shadow on the sail,
clear as an ultrasound silhouette
held by her vessel.

Watching the Dark

Dark strangles more than time.
It threads between our collars and throats, swells itself
to still breath. Inhale again and it's black,
so black it seems lighter with eyes closed.

All we have to pull us back is wind
on a cheek, or the neck, faint enough to be missed.

It's difficult not to feel resentful at four in the morning.
Anything for bunk and blanket, softened
by sleep, the off-watch and dreams

of home with its people
who know nothing of this and will never understand,
so these hours will blacken beyond recall.

The slow shift of constellations revolves around silence,
gateways and channels to nowhere.

At least cloud provides warmth.
And offers the thrill of a star jewelling through.

RICHARD WOTTON

The Language of Swallows

The broad, wooden door off the street creaks open,
scattering shadows from a cool archway,
scissors on stone:
quickquickquick! as they swerve
past our faces, swooping up to the rafters
and a row of heads that swivel as we enter.

Perched on the vine that shelters the courtyard,
they reel off a tongue-twisting twitter and trill
so we almost hear words;
they gossip until nightfall,
turning at times as if to include us,
or comment on the weekend's new arrivals.

Half-woken by their babble from the stairwell
to the blur of unfamiliar furniture,
we dream in answer,
but as the air curdles
into whitewashed walls and cafe shadows
the language of swallows dissolves into giggles.

Three Sketches about Reading
(Totoya Hokkei 1770–1850)

Distracted by a Flock of Birds

Fly away, scholar!
Trail the air between your toes!

High overhead already
cranes call out of sight.

A finger on the page,
thoughts over the horizon,

you outrace tomorrow,
lying in the long grass.

Burning the Midnight Oil

My eyes slow to the age of the untiring night.
The lamplight leans to ward me, flickering.
We are its conspirators, the wind and I.

We brush the letters, and they dance
across the shadows and the silence
in delirious clarity.

The space between them fills my sight.
The bare page shivers. How my ears sing!

Woman Walking as She Reads

A salmon's flank of silk turns with her,
plumes her on the cusp of movement,

ibis poised, intent, a message
waning to the curves of brow and cheek,

the letter's arc beneath her lips,
parted, silently pronouncing

sound grasped in the stroke of brush,
in the plunge and rise of a line:

her bare neck exactly tensed
to a deluge of dark hair withheld.

Gradus ad Parnassum

Follow the road uphill as far as a walled parterre
Lined with the busts of those believed to haunt the summit.

Here you could rest and drink from chattering fountains,
Share in the warmth of indiscriminate sunshine.

Here your path appears to turn back, curving downhill
Into the mountainside. The slope above is untamed;

If any routes lead upwards, they are merely tracks
Beaten through the bushes by those who have lost their way.

If the wind-whistling heights, where none stay for long,
Still call to you, follow the path into shadow.

As your senses grow accustomed to the darkness,
Look for curving terraces cut into the rock.

Do not be afraid to enter the arena
If what you bring is yours by gift and mastery,

The crowd will unbar the gate on the other side
Once you have fought the beast to their satisfaction.

But the terraces are bare
And the arena is empty

What choice do you have? Step forward and speak.

Distance

Ideas from the paintings in the "Caves of the Thousand Buddhas", Dunhuang, Western China, and "The Hunt in the Forest" by Paolo Uccello

It depends where you are
in the picture. Mountains
are so far away, but
a pine's branches close in.

The river descends marked
by points of boats – and spills
in its own green just by
the outcrop of my face.

It's not Uccello's advance
from the colours of the hunt,
measured, into death – or
the silence of dark woods.

It's not his last deer running
where perspective thins to lines.
It's not his one loose hound,
and then invisible things.

It is the shift travellers
discover when their gaze moves
from peaks to the dropping path
that aches the feet downhill.

It is the freedom of the eye
to insist. It is the mind's
adjustment to the world:
the world composed by eyes.

Ash

Regent's Canal near Limehouse, a December Monday

Ash seems under every particle of light
even where colours are their brightest.
Grey smoulders under the housing blocks,
char and powder mark the uneven grass,
the reeds. Coots dip in cinders on the canal.
I don't mean to turn back. I don't mean
to turn back into the flare of day ending
over the city, as if the towpath crumbled
at the blows of my feet, leaving a void
that slowly filled with water: canals, river,
tributaries, docks stringing together
as towers subside, cars choke, trains drown.
I do not mean to turn back, to see the veil
drawn over the collapsing networks – or the veil
drawn back, baring forest and an undergrowth
spoken in a hundred languages of birds.
Under my feet is ash, what's redeemed of fire.

Plants in Floodwater

Green, upraised
they seem englassed
on the verge
of chorus, the song
left hung
on leaf tips.

If summer comes
and they are not ploughed in
they might still have music.

HÉLÈNE CARDONA

Allegro Ma Non Troppo

Alone in silence.
Alone in the center of myself.
Alone saturated by darkness.
My aunt, the queen of blur,
won't give proper recollections
but I know how my mother died.
Alone in the center of herself.
The journey of the Fool is still mine,
salamander yearning to be salmon,
dueling sleepless haunted nights.
From the other side of the Atlantic,
I know how my mother released herself from pain.
How she sat on the edge of the tub,
head tilted, unruly auburn hair,
whole life floating by her,
gathering last thoughts
before joining my father in final embrace,
her smile ultimate legacy of safe passage.
The night is friend and foe,
I pray to all gods.
I remember, my body a container
filled to the brim with extreme sensation.
I remember, memory tricked
by imagination, the sweetest sting ever.
I remember what did exist,
what I created, how it all blends
till I emerge from the waking dream
unsure of what I lived
as my heart unleashed explodes.

Of Spies and Alchemy

The sand is God, bold, gigantic, regal,
ancient beaches made of dunes with views like the Alps.
I land on the mountain, know it
as a place to live on, higher than anything.
The coin is practical, necessary thinking, goes anywhere.
My value is not so easy to measure.
I change into other forms,
the alchemy of rubbing with intent,
a milkshake consumed, sensual disappearance,
become the drinker,
maintain equilibrium in the mind,
fairy tale ogre, assured, particular.
I should collapse.
I remain bound by different laws,
miraculous in consistency.
In a world of deceit, I'm for hire.
What I do for play, they do for life.
I assume any identity, except the odd one.
I want you to see me because we're the same.
Their code is only one agency,
caught up in a subtle form of control.
I have morals, don't want to report to anyone,
no choice but to make my own choices.
A funny thing, I enjoy the challenge,
it makes me happy.
I'm a hundred years old.
Life has so much more energy than pot-pourri,
it's here to experience and honor.
It doesn't look like much,
a container beyond the obvious surface.

Of Love and Poetry

I walk on the beach, in the ocean, on stones.
They stimulate my feet, dig into the flesh, remind
me I'm alive. I am spent. It's low tide. The water
is invigorating. Keep breathing, I tell myself. Keep
my feet on the ground. Stay connected to the earth
and myself. Don't leave.

I see myself as a kid on the beaches of Ibiza, picking
up stones with my cousin and painting them. I used to
look up to her because she was older. I'd observe her
getting ready and dressed up to go out. It seemed strange
to me. I felt, I'll always be the same. I'll never wear
make up or kiss a boy. Nothing's ever been what I thought
it would be.

I told my dad I'd return to Ibiza with him, the poet, go back
to the island where he was born and where they worship him,
share the same language, where they know and appreciate
him, where they interview and publish him, where he signs
autographs at the cafes. He sends me articles, photographs,
poems. He wants to know how he looks. I tell him, you had
to smoke in this one. They asked me to, he answers.

It's hard to know the truth. He might've showed up with a
cigarette and they said, keep it. I've always been touchy about
that. I've always hated it. I had never seen him cry until my
mom died. Last year he sent me one of his first books,
originally dedicated to his parents, and retrieved after his
mother died. He wrote this dedication to me, *Con el cariño y
el amor que todo lo trasciende, en lo que el ser humano se plasma
y en su plenitud alcanza la inmortalidad.* With the tenderness and
love that transcend it all, in which human beings are molded,
and so in their plenitude they reach immortality.

With it was a black and white photograph of my mother Kitty,
receiving from king Paul the trophy she won as rowing
champion of Greece. I too like rowing. I used to rent a boat
anywhere, in Paris, Germany, Austria. The trophy is now in

Madrid. She is so young in this photo. I can feel her energy, her eagerness, her strength, her love for life, her ability to accomplish anything.

She told me many times about love, about her love for me. I remember waking up one morning in Paris, and there she stood, in the light and shade, her arms extended toward me. We hugged. She a vision stepped out of the merging of my conscious and unconscious minds. She was courting me like a messenger. I could feel eons of emotions bottled up inside her, about to get unleashed. I was wondering what was going on. We didn't hug very often. I was tapping into a bottomless depth and getting dizzy. She was trembling. I became uncomfortable and concerned. I sensed her immense love and affection, how unconditionally she loved me.

Once I was asked who loved me the most. I was brought to tears just thinking of her. There had been so many misunderstandings because she held such high standards for me. I knew she wasn't able to communicate into words what was at the core of her being, what was corroding her. I knew she was keeping something from me. I knew she was afraid.

When I pulled away, she kept her arms extended to me, as she walked backwards to the door, as if she had to go somewhere, pulled by an invisible force, creating an energy field between us that would never be destroyed, thicker and denser than anything else in the room. She said before turning around, *only when I am no longer around, will you really know how much I loved you.* She repeated it like a mantra. She let go of the powerful rubber band that held us. It hit me in the heart and blinded me. I was so mad at her. I didn't know it yet, but my world had started crumbling down.

Pain is the great teacher. It strips the ego, the persona, only leaves consciousness, floating there, seeing beyond the mundane, allowing transcendence. It wipes out all unnecessary attachments, cleanses, purifies, enables to perceive a different reality.
What I seek is transformation.
Kitty opened a doorway for me.

In Dreams

Hélène Cardona. *Dreaming My Animal Selves / Le Songe de mes Âmes Animales.* Knockeven: Salmon Poetry, 2013. 79 pp. ISBN 978-1-908836-39-7, €12.00 pb.

Kate Fox. *Fox Populi.* Middlesbrough: Smokestack Books, 2013. 127 pp. ISBN 978-0-9571722-5-8, £7.95 pb.

Annie Finch. *Spells: New and Selected Poems.* Middletown, CT: Wesleyan UP, 2013. 215 pp. ISBN 978-0-8195-7269-1, US$30.00 hc, ISBN 978-0-8195-7363-6, US$16.99 pb.

Alison Brackenbury. *Then.* Manchester: Carcanet, 2013. 94 pp. ISBN 978-1-84777-118-6, £9.95 pb.

Hélène Cardona's *Dreaming My Animal Selves / Le Songe de mes Âmes Animales* is a work written in English and then translated into French by the author. Cardona's antece-

dents are certainly exotic; born in Paris to a Greek mother and an Ibizan father, she seems at home in many languages and many countries. Amongst the prefatory puffs – of which there are a significant number – the poet Thomas MacCarthy remarks "it is always a risky business for a poet to self-translate: it may seem like wanting both the work of art and the reader's response." Exactly how this is so is unclear. Well-translated work takes on another life in its new language, and surely the multi-lingual author with a foot in both camps occupies a privileged position with regard to the ability to convey meaning in the most precise and appropriate idiom possible? It would seem, from that point of view, the least risky of all possible worlds. The bilingual edition is interesting, but the poems must stand or fall as complete poems in either language; these are not macaronics. And indeed, the poems in this collection do concern themselves explicitly with movement, shape-shifting and liminal states of consciousness. As Cardona writes in "Dancing the Dream", "This is a story of flight, / a story of roots, / a story of grace. / I am the wandering child." (41)

The tone of these poems is often breathless, enraptured, and to borrow a phrase once used by Charles Tomlinson brilliantly to describe the poetry of Marina Tsvetaeva, 'self-wearing'. They are for the most part short lyrics and they frequently run the risk of being overbalanced by the weighty abstractions Cardona favours: "Subtle feminine power creates a magnificent / universe, rich soil, / Edenic mythological birds / and trees blooming in apotheosis'. ("Cornucopia", 33) What one longs for, amidst all of this high-flown mythology, is concrete detail, close observation, originality of eye. What is an embodied example of that "subtle feminine power"? In what way can that power be demonstrated, shown to us, rather than abstractly asserted? Cardona's work betrays a debt to the European tradition of poetic modernism, the kind of luminous fluidity found in Valery or Rimbaud, for instance. But their crystalline discipline of metre and form is not in evidence here; Cardona favours short unrhymed lines and free forms. There is a pantoum, "Peregrine Pantoum / Pantoum pelerine" (26-27) in which the forward-inching demands of the form are put to good use, and it would be interesting to see how Cardona's verse would respond in general to the strictures of more conventional verse form, should she choose to move in that direction.

Kate Fox's *Fox Populi* comes laced with a defensiveness that, to a non-British reader, might seem puzzling. In her author's note she writes: "Many of these poems were written to be read aloud by me on the radio or on a stage. Sometimes that leads to me being called a performance poet or (mainly if arts funding is involved) a 'spoken word artist.' An alternative phrase for this, in certain circles, is 'not a proper poet'." Similarly, the book's back cover blurb sassily declares that *Fox Populi* is "the kind of poetry that doesn't ignore most people", the implication being that 'proper' poetry (whatever that is) *does* ignore most people. This partakes of a familiar narrative of social and cultural ex-

Fox Populi

poems by Kate **Fox**

clusion frequently associated with the north of England (Fox is originally from Bradford), and also a class-obsessed (and often entirely imaginary) argument between artists who self-identify as 'popular' and artists who don't, and aren't, and are thus labelled 'elitist', that dirtiest of dirty words. The opposite of 'elitist,' in this scale of value, is 'accessible', which is officially a Good Thing. But a shelf is accessible, a poem is not. The question is whether these poems subvert the stereotypes or simply reinforce them. Often Fox teeters precariously between both positions. "Our Ends in the North", for instance, is an affectionate and funny look at the North-South divide, after an 'apocalypse' which is not described:

> On the second day I was on the bus
> when there was a bang and all the lights went out –
> and there was a chorus,
> of 'Call this an Apocalypse? I felt nowt.' (13)

The stereotype here is one of true grit, of doughty Northerners who are unfazed by anything, even the end of the world: "Grimsby hasn't looked this good since / the Germans redecorated" (13), but that's about it in terms of nuance.

Elsewhere, as in "Gardeners", a more subversive and satirical voice is in evidence: "They say, for people like us, / it's the best place to see what you can do, / it's where it's at. / But it just makes me think / my garden'll never look like that." (74) Fox sends up the class and geographical debate while at the same time being an uneasy participant in it. Most of the poems included in this volume, as the cover blurb also declares, occupy a position between "stand-up comedy and sit-down poetry." Along with the belly laughs, there are some well-observed and very personal poems. "Heirloom" deftly details a difficult family situation: "I wasn't entitled to my father's name / but I asked to keep his hat" (22); while "Threshold", "His Version" and "We Are Not Stones: a Glosa" describe a fraught relationship, albeit in very veiled terms. "Pelt" is a surreal excursion in linked images, beginning with "I am being driven to the airport / by one of Finland's only stand up comedians" (29) and moving by way of a fox fur-wearing Finnish poet to the pleasingly mysterious image of a "white animal scrabbling / out from under the creaking skins, / scaling the inside of the box / and scurrying urgently away." (30) Ultimately, the voice that emerges from *Fox Populi* is funny, poignant, and very likeable. Fox is in an honourable tradition of comic, and yes, 'popular' English verse. To worry about whether or not she is a 'proper poet' would seem to miss the point.

"I am proud to define myself as a woman poet", (xi) writes Annie Finch in the preface to her volume of new and selected poems, *Spells*. "… my ambition is to create a body of work for a re-emerging matriarchal culture." (xii) The poems in this volume appear in reverse chronological order, with a selection of newer poems at the beginning and the whole unreeling back to Finch's 1982 collection *The Encyclopaedia of Scotland*. There are then two separate sections, "Performance Works" and "Translations" which have a more conventional chronological structure. Finch's ambition and optimism about that re-emerging matriarchal culture is everywhere in evidence in this collection; there is a strong sense of female identity in these poems, as well as an evidently committed engagement with the work of other women writers visible in her translations from the work of

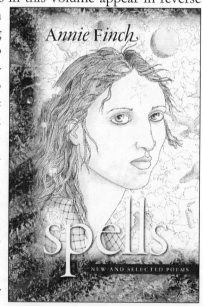

Anna Akhmatova and the French Renaissance poet Louise Labé. Finch has comprehensively raided the myth kitty, re-examining female roles in classical myth or the Judeo-Christian myth of origins, as in the unsettling "Another Pregnant Woman Remembers Incest":

Wailing, Cassandra came over the trees where we
lay, man and woman, and opened our eyes. We were
tired with the touch of the still-turning planets, and
tired with our dreams and the murders we knew (we had
kept generations of murder within us, and
now I was growing a murderer too). (99)

Similarly, "The Furious Sun in Her Mane" is a sequence of poems
which re-imagines a narrative for mythological figures as diverse as
Eve, Coatlique and the syncretised Celtic/Christian Brigid. But this is
not just a political position for Finch – indebted though she undoubt-
edly is to her coming of age as a writer during the second wave of
American feminism in the 1970s. Mythology underpins this collection
in ways that are much more intrinsic and intimate. In "Poems for the
Wheel of the Year" she writes of the Celtic year from Samhain to the
Wiccan Mabon (Finch is a Wiccan), using song and incantation to examine the ancient cycles in a register that is celebratory:

The sun, rich and open,
stretches and pours on the bloom of our work.

In the center of the new flowers,
a darker wing of flower

points you like a fire.

Point your fire like a flower. (44)

The impression given is of a poet for whom such preoccupations are a
natural part of life and central to her world view.

In evidence throughout this volume is Finch's passionate in-
volvement with the nuts and bolts of poetic craft, her abiding fascination with the variety of poetic form and metre. This forms a pleasingly
intuitive harmony with the mythological interests detailed above. The
rigours of metre, of patterned speech, connect, Finch seems to be im-
plying, to something ancient in the human psyche; as she puts it,
"patterned language that invites readers to experience words not just
in the mind but in the body." (Preface, xi) To this end, *Spells* contains
an astonishing variety of experiments in poetic form and tone, including sonnets, villanelles, elegies, longer narrative poems, short lyrics,
verse drama, libretti, and other intricately rhymed and patterned

shapes. But the familiar incantatory tone is seldom far beneath the surface of these poems, to a greater or lesser degree of effectiveness, depending on the subject. Finch frequently favours the no-holds-barred commitment of full end rhyme, which fits with her aims, of course, but can occasionally sound a little quaint. In the very fine poem "Elegy for My Father" some of these energies converge with considerable success in a moving description of a deathbed scene. One is reminded of Emily Dickinson, whose presence haunts these pages, but Finch's vision here is less shattered, less existentially appalled by the act of witness:

> Night, take his left hand, turning the pages.
> Spin with the windows and doors that he mended.
> Spin with his answers, patient, impatient.
> Spin with his dry independence, his arms
> warmed by the needs of his family, his hands
> flying under the wide, carved gold ring, and the pages
> flying so his thought could fly. His breath slows,
> lending its edges out to the night.

Here, the soothing, incantatory tone of Finch's verse is at its most moving and apposite. *Spells* bears witness to a considerable body of work and an impressive commitment to the traditions of poetry across a poetic career that spans four decades.

Formal preoccupations are also very apparent in *Then*, Alison Brackenbury's eighth full collection of poems (she also published a Selected Poems with Carcanet Press in 1991). It could be said that this is poetry that minds its manners, it is a poetry of careful observation, of graceful cadences and painstaking craft. But that would be to understate its cumulative power; Brackenbury does not shy away from difficult subjects, and her craft is flexible and adaptable enough to encompass historical subjects, descriptions of her rural childhood, acute observations of the natural world, a satirical response to a remark by Pete Doherty (of Babyshambles fame), poems about the First World War, and the recent severe floods in her home county of Gloucestershire, among many other themes. The collection opens with a remembered flood in "The Trent rises, 1947":

> When you heard the water whisper
> in Crown Yard and Sailor's Alley,

when your husband saw the river
no longer lazy – swollen, free;
what did you grab, to take with you upstairs?
What would I take with me? (9)

ALISON BRACKENBURY *Then*

This is the first of a number of poems set in the Lincolnshire of the poet's childhood, or even earlier, recalling the inhabitants of a now vanished agricultural world: "Grandmother's mother's desk / from the legendary lost farm / was salvaged by my parents / from dog food, sheep salves, grime.' ("Left", 19) There is a characteristic liveliness and empathy on display here; one never feels that these are museum pieces or exercises in historicism. Among the poems in this section are several about the poet's parents in old age. These often difficult subjects are handled with a sensitivity and lightness of touch resulting in large part from the cool, tactful distance afforded by her skilful use of rhyme and metre:

My mother dead. What did she leave?
Dry days of frost, a weight to grieve.
The dead wake us with worries,
sour milk, the universe.

("Fruit in February", 26)

Much as in Annie Finch's work, the regular rhymes and cadences of the verse have a lulling, consolatory quality to them, although Brackenbury has little truck with incantation. Her take on formalism is closer, one senses, to the rationalism of Frost's description of poetry as "a momentary stay against confusion".

Elsewhere in the collection, Brackenbury's acute sense of the natural environment is striking. Poems such as "Bombus" and "Harvest" are touched by the mystery of the natural world, even as they describe and celebrate aspects of it. "Lapwings" recalls Keats' characterisation of the nightingale as "immortal bird", as the poet meditates on the reassuring, if frequently ignored, continuity in nature:

> I only knew them gone
>
> when, out of a sad winter, one returned.
> I heard the high mocked cry 'Pee – *wit*', so long
>
> cut dead. I watched it buckle from vast air
> to lure hawks from its chicks. That time had gone. (37)

And yet, underlying this meditation is a sense of anxiety at change, an environmental awareness that is never dogmatic or strident, but is nevertheless persistently adumbrated. This comes to a head in the book's final, six-part section, entitled "Flood". There is a pleasing sense here of things coming full circle, from the flood-themed opening poem of the collection, but these poems describe a tragic situation and a growing problem: "We are made of water. But we forgot" ("Flood", 87) and "The rivers rise, the doomed pumps hum, / the walls are down, the waters come / to Munich, Paris, London." ("Review", 92)

Nevertheless, despite the anxieties darkening the edges of these poems, Brackenbury's is ultimately a celebrant's voice. In the final poem of the collection, "No", we are reminded that, despite everything:

> Nothing in all history
> can reach to take your hand from me,
> the dark, the rain's gift, O
> we should be glad. (93)

In order to assert this "we should be glad" the poet has worked through a first stanza couched in negatives: "No one is ever good enough, / or kind enough / ... No one is good." (93) Such moments of affirmation, therefore, are far from facile; rather, this work implies that they are hard-won through experience instead of simply claimed, and this finely-judged collection makes Brackenbury's witness to them eminently believable.

ANNIE FINCH

First Moon

Threaded alive with our shadows,
chaining our shadows of daughters,
moving beyond our beginnings,

pulling our spiralling borders,
carrying on your beginnings,
moon linking our daughters

through choices, and still more beginnings:
moon of our daughters, and mothers.
These are our bodies' own voices,

the powers of each of our bodies,
unbroken, begetting, and threading
through the flowers of each of our bodies.

KATE FOX

The Dormant Poet

This poem is like a supermarket employee
who has been taught to ask if you've had a nice day
but not to care about the answer.

It cannot let go of some anxiety while you link
a rubber mat squeaking as it is positioned
under spouting water at the top of the log flume,

the suddenly clear view of the road behind you
on the return journey
after the banana boxes have been carried out.

It has relinquished lines
about a dangling string, an outstretched hand,
a dot in the shape of a child.

None of it as effortless
as the daily miracle of the pillow
whose exact moment of occurrence
is evasive as an electron under a microscope.

We've found out sleep is to allow
the day's toxins to flush through your brain
like water through pipes,

interstitial cavities extend
like gaps between words
at the end of a speech,

our limbs splayed
like the branches of monkey puzzle trees.

@ Norbert

Our dog knows that air is memorable and his nose tells truths;
which way the sparrows, shoes and shopping bags went,
that a subtle new bouquet has arrived in the field
where he snuffles grass scents as if they are a fine salad
laid out just for him.
He knows that days are plenty wide enough
to greet every being who passes
and fixing cocoa eyes on sausages
can bring them miraculously closer.
He knows the dimensions of the last space on the settee,
how to paddle his paws to slot in
and punctuate his flow with easy sleep.
He knows to dash to my feet when he hears the metallic pop
of his treat tin lid,
the rustle of my coat as I slide it off the hook.
He knows I'm on my way back before I do,
his bottom waggling like a bee high on pollen

just as excited whether it's been five minutes or five days
since I moved out of his view,
Our dog doesn't know that his days as a quick black cloud
will ever end,
that repetition is not always the same as prediction,
that his wet paw prints blur metaphors I have written him into.
He doesn't know that I'm not in the house
as he thumps his feather duster tail
to the sound of my voice on the phone.
That curled nose to tip into an @
he has become my sign for home.

MARC HARSHMAN

Running the Chances

Was it just the rattle of the old pick-up,
its whimpering squeal of brakes
that made me think of you?
I was sitting on a park bench stranded
between two mountains, and unblessed with a map.
The fortitude of stones and gravity lay upon me.
I was feeling almost lonely, a lost star,
when a distant whistling of an old tune
crawled its way into that last hour of light.

The distance between two points is some kind of number,
cousin to truth but here I was, autumn well advanced,
and not only was there no toothbrush but
my cell wouldn't work so how could I know
anything without its electric pulse?
I remember you telling me there is more to
everything than meets the eye
and so the sky rose up to meet me,
large words in crayon littered across the landscape.

And the children on those bicycles talked
with hay in their voices and spider webs of
memories from the long ago. It was time to light
candles in the big house and pour burgundy into
the stiff hands of our smoky glasses. It was time
to untie the skiff and float into the umber sheen
of an icy lake where words and numbers coalesced
in a singularity adamant as graphene and viscous as sorghum.

I would spend the night here, bend my circles
within yours, defeat biometrics with sleek interlockings
of kisses and a sexual science unknown to our parents.

And when we came down the silken stairs to earth,
the morning would have arrived renewed
within the green cradle of these ancient mountains,
and we no longer lonely, but whistling as if
there were children somewhere who knew our names
and if we'd run our chances, well, we'd have no complaint.

Return Ticket

John sat reading his Bible, a joint
in one hand, a glass of red,
cheap red, in the other, a tin of tuna
centering the table – our shared lunch –
he lifted his head, wondering – perhaps
I did, as well – whether
the two ends would ever meet, about
the tie that binds, whether the circle
would be unbroken, whether Bojangles
ever really danced, while Kitty purred
in one corner and I sat in the other
chanting the names of each pebble
we'd adopted in case of Kitty's demise.
We weren't the only ones in danger of overdosing:
the catnip flourishing under

the pot's frondy leaves had left her
comatose after her hour chasing circles.

A jolly chessboard would be sitting on the floor.
A game of chance I insisted despite
his winning again and again.
He'd been to heaven or so he told me
and the return ticket he kept buried
in the drawer with condoms
and roach clips and blue rags.
But even the acid wouldn't dislodge
his itinerary or his visions.
Cards close to his chest, an old man
of the mountains at twenty-two.
I'd join him for strolls through forests
we worshipped in the abstract
while scheming to get laid.
He'd win there, too. Despite his oddities,
he knew the talk and I never did.
The women flocked. I hid.
The cat died. The pebbles, though we tried
calling them by name, never warmed
to us and soon, names forgotten,
disappeared under the broom
onto College Street where the new children
never stopped arriving. He was legendary
by then … and me? I'd gone straight, headed east.
It seemed a good direction to go.
He emptied his drawers and told me later
that the ticket had gone missing.
He had, however, saved one last pebble and
placing it on his tongue, found himself –
he swore to this – speaking like a cat
coherently summoning his pride to follow him
all the way to Maine and Indiana.
Maybe it's true. He's asked me about that ticket.
I never lie but sometimes, sometimes at night,
after a meal of tuna and wine, I like to tell a story.
And John, he shows up, every time, wings
at his shoulders, joint at his lips.

Sonnets

I
From Scott's Journals

Saturday; at Camp, I scattered some oats.
Weary Willy has kept the course so far
and the ponies seem to be strong. The clouds
are thin and rolling in Antarctic pink.
Saw James Pigg, Michael, and Snatcher up ahead
and we drew up within an hour to rest.
The men are pink and soft and kind in chaff
and laugh between the quiet creaking ice.

At Shambles Camp we gave ourselves some sleep.
The snow like sand, loose upon the surface,
holds us back as the seasons hurry on.
We had our best hoosh yet – a pemmican
horse-meat stew – which really heats the belly.
Canzone, i' sento già stancar la penna.

II
From The Pillow Book of Sei Shōnagon

An earthen cup
        an ill woman in the eyes of her lover
a torn-up letter put together again
        the inside of a cat's ear.

the mayfly and the firefly
        priests. fruit. horses as well as oxen.
silver tweezers that still pluck the hair
        women of the lower classes.

paradise
on an old man's back
the sound of comb-teeth snapping.

the seventh month
(when it is cool) reading
my poem in another girl's notebook.

III
From Velásquez

I have drawn the same queen a thousand times
and she still won't laugh at my joke about
her shrivelled hand. Not that I don't like it.

She comes, shuts the cold out, as Browning said,
and hangs her coat up on an empty peg.
Desire would take me, if I could desire.

I have set everything in its right place,
adjusted the futon, counted the plums,
allowing the light to polish their sides.

She sits, holding her hair in the good hand,
nothing in the other. I watch her grasp
the situation, counting up the plums.

We are not slow to seek out our own kind.
I have drawn this same queen a thousand times.

IV
From The Medieval Scene

The clack of the carriage chasing the bell's
chirrup.
          The burning urge to arrest smells
                    on the page.
The mirror within an inch of the eye.

Kick me
if ever I disappoint the image
or break the sabbatizare
I am clearly
an apple on the slow-moving ass's
back. Drawn up the hill / whatever pleases.

The clack of the trap chasing the ass moves
me as I think it should move you. The grooves

in this hillside signs of our obedience.

V

A Sketch of John Dowland in Denmark

Through pipes and contraptions
I come to you,
from a cellared world
my angular intention

aspires. What's hellish is
hidden.
Only the beauty
survives.

Through distance and exile
I came to you,
and wormed my way into

the core. Once insidious, now
ridiculous; singing
through pipes and contraptions.

VI

Pavane: Anubis

I give the green-fruit
try for transcendence.

        These the gifts, this the dance
        those the people believing.

I long as corn
jackal-headed corn,

        scale the heart, feed the dogs
        those the people believing.

Thin limbs
        with skirt and flail
                foot following flute,
the dancers part
        ethic and image
                those the people believing.

VII

From Cavalcanti

A lady is pregnant, so I must sing
of some wild passion – the saleable type,
love, straight as a needle, blunt at the tip –
an accident, and a well plotted thing.
It grows, from the damaged area
the part, behind the eyes, where thoughts reside.
It is, despite belief, a parasite –
devours reason, exudes hysteria.
You remember – what you have never known –
a crimson cloth, a sentimental song,
it spreads its choler, along the phloem,
causing men to bark, when they mean to sing.
There is no cure, but it can show mercy,
infect another, or kill you quickly.

[88]

VIII
From Andrew Marvell

The poet in the garden counts the shoots
like syllables, the vegetable language
slowly forms. Sibyl in a bamboo cage
contorts the meaning in the scattered fruits.

Every thought is an attack on nothing,
a forage for the hedgerow deity.
Words abound but do not bite their meaning.
The blue tit waits, prepared for longer play.

Then memory, like a hard rime, returns,
says, go in fear of the organic form.
The garden disappears inside the worm
and the poet, spat out, is forced to leave.

Parts of the feast remain. Tuber and blooms.
Thoughts into words harden – tight little tombs.

SCOTT ELDER

The Trade

I saw you in the fields trading the wings.
What did the rooks leave in return?
A claw? A broken beak?

And what was that shriek?
You were staring at some furry thing,
small and grisly in your hand. Dead still it was.

Are you better now? You look so pale.
What do you see? Look at me!
The sky is empty. Empty!

And the harbor too.
All the freighters are sunk but one,
and you on the deck with your precious cargo:

two broken spokes to a rusty wheel.
Is that what they left you?
Was that the deal?

Here's my hand. The wind is calling.
The lady of the wind
will carry us home.

View from a Garret Window

If you, my dear, were allotted
nine lives, then I inherited
eight of yours, and as many deaths.

When you closed your eyes
death rang the horizon.
A cloud bank trundled along its edge.

And now, in turn, in the circle's center,
the sun seeps in,
plunders darkness in swallows.

I close my eyes
in perfect time,
walk naked and without desire.

A cloud bank moves on forever,
leaving behind the memory of thunder
and gentle rain bathing the valley,

beating spring and autumn together
on cut stone tiles
and dusty window panes.

This House Is Alarmed

This is such a structure as was
Spoken into existence
In a dry storm when a humid air
Would hang fire, or so we would

Assume: of how a rain shot-blasts first
Then punctuates, a sun illuminate,
A cool breeze edit a hard-edged
Brick and Tile body text.

Prospective buyers are advised to interpret
Entrances and exits in context; windows
As eyes, then take a crack at deciphering
The rising chimney smoke; afterwards

Transcribing this revelation, for we know
There's a secret brewing in that saucer cloud
That has persisted overhead as if it were
An alien mothership about to give birth.

The Sky at Night

You gaze down from the highest building knowing
There is a text to be trawled from a whirlpool;

All the stars are 'denizens of the deep'
From the reddest to the bluest;

You supposed it were best to be a sardine
If fate should turn turtle and the big ships

Were out to get you; or a single ice-crystal
In the outer ring of Saturn or the titchiest

Slug of dilithium in the starship drive
While you were out on galactic business.

When is an ambassador nothing but background radiation?
Every nebula is a text forever reconsidering its options

Just as every space-cat might look at a Spock
Before going for broke in a brand new world,

In a continuum in which it is possible to pad up walls
Without being observed by a three-headed dog,

Camouflaged by the simplest wallpaper pattern;
Everything you are as binary inside a nautilus.

Freedom

Click here to enlarge.
Freedom waits with open arms.
For the privilege of getting airborne
There is a charge. You will pay the price for you know
The landscape beyond the door is yours even as
A phantom flits then goes abroad.

Click here to enlarge.
Freedom observes, as Christopher Robin
Plus the cast of Grimm and much besides
Will get educated should they get airborne
And pay the price beyond the door, their phantom
Going before them, going abroad.

Click here to enlarge.
Freedom knows the footfalls heard
Behind the door is the Prodigal returning,
Charged and suitably repentant, by now understanding
His secret life was never to defy a pricey gravity
But he's established that Freedom is a person!

Yes Freedom is a person who would fall from the moon
In what would seem to be a suicidal parabolic
Until the observers down below see the play
And seize the moment and know the price is paid:
What is the Grand Canyon to a phantom flitting?
The doors revolving, space-stations waltzing to Strauss?

ROBERT LEACH

The Fish

My hand holds
A silver slippery fish.
It flaps, slaps
My palm, frantic
For the water of life.

You too can have a fish
And feel its scales
Spank your skin.

Its life fades
Like dry twilight,
But now I can cook my fish,
Toast its brilliant sides,
Roast it ruddy
Over flames which puff and hiss

And taste the flesh –
Though what I appreciate
May not be quite
What you enjoy.

Still,
We both are satisfied
With this meal.

In Search of Happiness

A Russian Dream

Hearing the Soviet State Folk Ensemble's
Cantering *Kalinka* –
Presto! Presto! Prestissimo! Then
Ritardando! Lento! Stop! – it's not

The tang of raspberries
On the tongue, nor the sly smell
Of conjured pine forests,
Nor even the memory
Of the Moscow Oblast's silver birches
Which wets my eyelash – it's

The quickening rasp
Of oversized metro carriages,
The crouched black vacancy without
Meeting tired yellow light bulbs within - it's

The clanking slowdown
Approaching stations big with
Carved wheat sheaves in the arms of
Carved peasants, and the
Traipsed wetness, smeared like tears,
Across the fake marble platform – it's

The crammed-in people with heavy greatcoats,
The scarlet-lipped and fur-collared women,
The men with parcels, brief cases pouched
And baggy as their faces,
The pale students with their
Endless webs of spidery Cyrillic
On thin yellow pages – it's

Osterezhno! Dveri zakryvaetsa!
And the train lurching off again,
Accelerating into darkness.

Notes:

In Search of Happiness: the title of a comedy of 1957 by Viktor Rozov, later made into the film *Noisy Day*.

Kalinka: very popular folk song especially with large 'official' Soviet choirs, telling of the sweet raspberries in the garden and the fine pine forests. It is noted for the way in which it speeds up and slows down in performance.

"Oblast": Communist administrative district.

Osterezhno! Dveri zakryvaetsa!: 'Take care! The doors are closing!' spoken over the tannoy at the end of every station stop.

June Afternoon

Sky – blue lid
On the sun-sloshed afternoon,
The lane's tarmac black and melting
Just a little at the edges,
And the bursting hedges –
Two ranks of green generals with their chests thrust out,
Bemedalled with cow parsley, tormentil, buttercups.

We cruised carelessly
Down the old cartway,
Round the bend,
And braked:
A cow munching the grass verge,
Its backside blocking our way
Like a piebald five-bar gate.

It swung its head towards us,
Eyes misty grey, tongue pink and dangling.
It wasn't exactly frightened, but
It flounced its head with ponderous panic,
As if it knew it disturbed the order of things
Just a little
That June afternoon.

F e r m a t a

She held the high note, or held what she had,
as a gift the dark sea of gentility
could not refuse …

                    The gowns rocked with the wave,
ballasted to their velvet seats. Had you
been deaf, you might as easily have suspected
a sudden epidemic of hemorrhoids.
The tuxes riffled as some sleeves rotated
that eyes might steal glances at watches, masked
by cuffs of sleeves; other arms rose like a
baton striking an inconspicuous upbeat
(their watches closer to the heart, but harder
to get to, on fobs in stylish waistcoat pockets)
then completed the cycle in a downbeat of
unvoiced, attentive, polite desperation.
The ensemble of the audience, then, was still
as mice in a tempest, reluctant to
scurry, so as not to enrage the storm.

Her accompanist nodded, signaling release,
but she did not let go. (Iván remarked
he'd never seen a soprano smile so well
on "O" before. *Or for so long,* said Carlotta.)

Later in private she explained the true
liberation implied at each fermata,
the trust required. He kept playing for her.

She wore light satin gowns with gloves and pearls –
even rehearsing her cadenzas and portamenti –
but was invited to perform only
that once. She's planning to tour Europe soon.

Garden

He husbanded his wife as rocky ground
was often "husbanded". He was a good
gardener, and did everything he should
to harvest the ripest fruits and brightest flowers.
She had legs, though, and liked to walk around,
not lie like some dumb flowerbed for him.
The gate's wrought iron latchkey seemed a grim
    containment of spring, to her. She
     began to stay away for hours,
         then days. *Where have you been,*
         he'd ask, then threaten to lock
         her out. Which he did, that fall,
         on confirming his suspicion.
By winter he unlocked the doors again
but she was gone. She sees him in the grocery
    from time to time. He doesn't talk,
but lives on, in that same old house, alone.
This spring his garden is plush and overgrown.

Poetry Salzburg Pamphlet Series 10

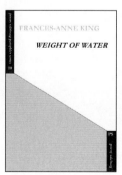

Frances-Anne King
Weight of Water
October 2013. 36 pp. ISBN 978-3-901993-44-2
£4.50 (+ 1.00 p&p), €5.50 (+ 1.00 p&p), US$8.00 (+ 1.50 p&p)

"Frances-Anne King's *Weight of Water* strikes a beautiful balance between mystery and disclosure, bravery and tact, the kind of tact which nonetheless keeps her zeal in place. What underpins the whole collection is not a commonplace 'accessibility', but her dignified restraint; the line is balanced and controlled, the vision never in question. It is a memorable first book."

Tim Liardet

DAVID MOHAN

Black Fields

Land lies fallow at Edge City,
untitled by lights. Electrics
have forgotten to forge their signature.
The slow fields wait like ink
in its well, passive, dreaming of
finding its character.

This is the neighbourhood of jet
beauty spots, the micro-districts
set against mountains, burghs
of teeming copse. Sometimes,
night trains pass, their faint sketch
rubbed by hours into a smudge.

The air is taut, lunar,
out here in drift and night
at the crest of a view nobody owns.
The eye struggles to find its horizon –
soon it climbs off the land
into the stars' sprawl of millions.

Vacuum

I like retraction, reversal
of the Hoover's stomach –
disembowelled it reveals
what's left to settle in a room.

I find pockets of lint,
cough-balls of fluff,
a static vest
of vacuous fabric;

what's through with happening;
the fall of dust become edit –
yarn bulbs of stuff,
a bolus strung out to a mess.

Unravelled, I relish strewing it,
returning it to the carpet,
to mattresses, polished surfaces,
like a mourner emptying ash.

JOHN WEDGWOOD CLARKE

Field Notes

Pen shadow, ink glisten –
curlew catch hold,
draw me from my burrow.

After the big blow
a hot battery of seaweed,
flies sugar-rushed.

Leeward high tide, no swell,
just the verb of bird
becoming merganser.

Torn water, gorse on fire –
cool celadon glaze
on the Eider's beak.

It's not my task to count them
and it is: I want
the stillness of numbers.

Empty houses, a moored yacht –
rain, bless my notebook,
make me put it away.

Dead Man's Fingers

Alcyonium digitatum

Just fear that's talking – it was never dead
and never man's; neither is it the sea's
dugs wrinkled with life, sucked out and hungry
to give suck, bursting to feed. But it does
look not quite unfamiliar; not *Hand*
of Doom, but something like, pimply and sprigged,
aflame with pale palms wavering to be
born from open pores in finger tips,
hands bursting through the category of hands
into astonishing holds. From the agg-
lomerate of barnacle and keel worm
flow digits of death milk, life milk, the sea's
curdled tongue filling a mouth that's playing
for time and would have it otherwise.

Gurnard

The glass flask
of its swim-bladder
came up too quickly;

overblown,
no one can let it down
lightly. Its squat pupil

deepens, cold
as the Atlantic by
that lump of engine

thrown in the lee
of The Gurnard
where the swell darkens,

our legs only floaters
in its blue-black eye.

Muzak

He's a black fedora throwback
(Jimmy Stewart dates Kim Novak)
well clock the shiny shoes
the silver collar-pin   her flouncy
taffeta   the spin they're in
the quick quick slow the
"I'm his sugar he's my beau"

He's seen the movies   does his best
despite the little raindrop eyes
and all the rest

He's found his Kim   his kindred soul
And when the party's over or the picture show
they'll hold hands at the bus stop though
he owns a car of sorts
Others randier (or maybe fonder)
head to car park back seat
Evie's BM   Josh's Honda

And what about the notes he sends her
(never phones) which she ties up
in ribbon bows

Sue Spink lets on she dated him
a year ago ("the great daft get
total dickhead wet wet wet")

Steve's mum insists she saw him
bare-arsed with the blonde
back of the chip shop shed
but who'd believe
a thing Steve's mother said

Then there's little Jethro
check-out kid at Tesco
swears the pair of them came
dolled up ballroom style
waltzing chin-high Viennese
all up and down the biscuit aisle

Golem

First articulate the clay as
trowelled sound
as meditation
Hereby raise
the mute word's
protégé
       mauled form
of marl and
uncrowned nouns
hitched diphthongs and
a prayerful consonance
botch artfully
as if
of ribbon tape and daisy-crepe but this

is shadow kabbala
pray *a* pray *e*
then *i* which sighs
and *o*

make life from sky (the word) and likewise
asphodel
       vermillion's there
and crepuscule
         cue yew (the *u*)
cue single
       linden
words words words
and mouth sounds gag for air

for blood and breath
parsed then / parsed now
Torah Tao
Rg Veda
Song of Babylon

con origins: the ums and ahs and
            dirt and letter-cards
            The Word as stars eu
            -karyotes
            then sheep and goats and
            candyfloss and one across
            and truth and hocus pocus
            chaos → logos

JULIE MACLEAN

Leopard Day
After a line by Pascale Petit

It's on a morning like this
        I find a shrike with
            the cramped feet of the bird-dead
lying on gravel
next to the kangaroo paw

I hold still in spite of fine drizzle
        soaking through my linen
        top   pick it up by its fan tail
witness to something pathetic & true
disappointed by dull plumage
        I think of its lost song

the way it stops me
        in the ringing

sitting at my desk, always doing
          Instinctively, I move into
my needled forest of she-oak
          camouflaged

               My eyes
become black slits squinting
          against the splintering sun casting
a shard haze   lighting me up

My feet become soft paws
          soft-padding through the jungle
my tail can't help itself

This minute I forget who I am
          that the claws scuffing
backbones
                    of skeleton leaves
scattering millipedes
          & hard bodies of primeval insect

will shake my morning's aria
          from the wattle   now ablaze

Was Red

Love happens
In back lanes sometimes
And school rooms

Only now
Remembering your
Cracked tooth smile

               The year when
               Elderberries stained
               Our pale hands

Jealousy
Changed the palette
Clouds turned green

Far far north
Grey wolf hunts moose calf
On tundra

Arctic fox
Goes piebald in winter
Cubs to feed

She hunts all
Day   Snowy owls
Swallowed in one

Reindeer cross
The last big river
When ice comes

When I'm gone
Dried by desert winds
Of the south

Think of me
When red stains appear
On your mouth

Boy with the Silver Earring

For Daniel

When he said
     that from a particular angle

rows of turbines in the ocean wind farm
     coming into Copenhagen

were the arms of Shiva, the way
     the blades waved, he was right

You Say Babel

The jigsaw puzzle on the table
Gets more chaotic as it grows.
The Bedford Hours, "The Tower of Babel",
Extends to where (its cover shows)
Assembled angels will lambaste
The efforts of our elbow grease
Until no parts remain where placed,
But lie re-scattered, every piece.
We're game. Our hushed, collective wiles
May spare us yet from abstruse babble,
The bedlam and the flying tiles
That always spell an end to Scrabble.

A Fable

An elephant was charging home to lunch,
Some plantains cradled in his trunk.
Mid-river, though, he dropped the bunch; they'd sunk.

He stamped, and in a russet rage, he thrashed
the water, till it danced and yellowed
and seemed to laugh, the more he splashed and bellowed.

He stopped and glared, reproving and irate,
At sloths who mumbled from a nearby tree,
Just wait, stop moving, wait and see, just wait.

He stared them into silence, bent and peered
And found he'd also stilled the stream's catharsis.
He spied his plantains as the surface cleared.

He grabbed them, slapped the river twice and left,
not deeming tree-sloths worth a quarrel.
But one slow voice called after him, bereft,
Come back, come back, we're working on a moral.

The Pearl Feeder

It was a rumor eighty years ago,
When movie studios were in their glory,
And if they gave the word to drop a veil
Over some vanished has-been and her story,
Not even friends-of-friends would tell your tale.
These earrings still speak eloquently, though.

She was an extra, just one of many girls,
Until a mogul noticed she'd a way
With beads, that seemed to light them from within.
And after that she didn't work a day
On film, but was demanded for her skin.
Rich women paid to have her wear their pearls.

Imagine growing old in someone's vault,
Where you'd report – your own depositary –
Be garlanded, then shut inside each day,
Entombed, as in an ancient reliquary,
Imparting luster while you dimmed away.
The town forgot and found no one at fault.

It might have been her heart and not neglect,
That killed her in a strong-room in the hills.
She died alone, though, no one in attendance
And certainly no one to help or grieve.
No truth to any whispers, I suspect –
At any rate, untouched by gossip mills –
that autopsy retrieved two ruined pendants
like these. Please take them with you when you leave.

Summoned Voices

Barbara Hardy. *Dante's Ghosts*. Walthamstow: Paekakariki Press, 2013. 58 pp. ISBN 978-1-908133-06-9, £12.50 pb.

Abegail Morley. *Eva and George – Sketches in Pen and Brush*. Hadlow: Pindrop Press, 2013. 61 pp. ISBN 978-0-9573290-3-4, £7.99 pb.

Frank Osen. *Virtue, Big as Sin*. San Jose, CA: Able Muse Press, 2013. 69 pp. ISBN 978-1-927409-16-9, US$17.95 pb.

Noel King. *The Stern Wave*. Cliffs of Moher: Salmon Poetry, 2013. 81 pp. ISBN 978-1-908836-33-5, €12.00 pb.

Mary O'Gorman. *Flames of Light*. Tralee: Doghouse, 2013. 56 pp. ISBN 978-0-9572073-8-7, €12.00 pb.

Something that is not quite tangible, but that many of us may recognise, is what makes picking up a collection of poems different from opening any other kind of book. There is the sense at once of the oral  dimension, and thus of being a listener, intent on catching a voice. And then of trying to isolate and distinguish it from those other voices which can be heard breaking in: the influences, the mentors and editors, benign or misguided, and sometimes the homogenized static of the workshop. Weaving between them, faint or overbearing or clear is the voice of the poems, not quite the same as the poet's own voice. Since poets on occasion invite in accents other than their own, or less justifiably borrow accents they have a dubious title to, poems choose their speakers. Reading these five books I was aware of numerous voices, and sometimes of silences; speakers are summoned but like Glendower's spirits from the vasty deep they do not always obey the invocation.

The abyss they are called from is a profound one, and in navigating it there are wide gaps to be crossed: gaps of time, of gender and of language. And in a sense also gaps of talent and originality, some of which can elicit that creative audacity which counts as talent in itself. In these collections, from England, America and Ireland, all but the last address the deep fault-lines. Barbara Hardy takes on Dante's *Commedia*, not as translator (a role that demands talent and courage enough), but as rewriter, arranging that supercosmic structure into a fifty-page collection of lyrics and drawings (the latter are by Kate Hardy and are lovely). She has form; a respected academic, she has done what literary academics aren't supposed to, publishing speculations about the later lives of Austen's Emma and George Eliot's Dorothea. Even so, the sheer impertinence of squaring up to Dante has to be admired; and his is a voice that speaks out loud and bold at her summons.

It's not that her choices are especially original. She follows not only Dante but the stream of commentators that begins six and a half centuries ago; she chooses the figures Macaulay's schoolboy would have known: Pier delle Vigne, Paolo and Francesca, Brunetto Latini, Casella, Belacqua. She captures the Dantean clarity in the Brunetto episode, in a version that comes close to a translation – so *of course* she scores a hit; in her poem on the Ugolino episode she chooses to sound like a smart critic which I think is a pity.

What would it be like for a reader who was not recalling Dante? It is an absence too vast for me to imagine, but I think anyone would catch the the vivid force in her remaking of the Brunetto encounter, both its accuracy in the last line and its paraphrase of

>   … the poet
> who saw the brilliant old sinner
>
> race off to his allotted share
> of hellfire
> with the alacrity not of a loser
> but a winner ("Reunion", 7)

Less august voices can also be borrowed. They may be marginal or suppressed, like so many voices of women over millennia. Eva Peter, who married George Grosz in 1916, met him when they were both art students. The poems in Abegail Morley's *Eva and George* do not reflect on the life and career she might have had; they allow her to comment on his art, politics, historical setting, their favourite pronouns "you" and "we":

you tell me of your
disillusion with Communism

how you live
in the shit of the world

in a country
that muffles art ("Tonight", 33)

The life of a terrific and terrifying artist is viewed from the periphery

**Eva and George —
Sketches In Pen and Brush**

Abegail Morley

where his wife is placed as observer; the drawings and photographs included in the book remind us of his genius, while the poems underline the extraordinary match between his view of the world as nightmare and the scary story actually unfolding in the history of Germany in his time. Since the book is based on historical fact it must pay tribute to hard realities. "Sometimes only the literal / Can express any generous truth" wrote my late friend, the Irish poet Pearse Hutchinson. Historical, literal truth has a claim on our attention, it has necessarily a public air, and a poet who is faithful to fact can import that public accent even when writing about the private lives of historical figures.

George Grosz's talent has made us see the German 1920s through his eyes and to see it with the urgency of hindsight. The drawings included here include "Vorstadt (Suburb)", where he shows his power of distortion, eerie playing with the two-dimensional, and his fascination with the vibrating screen that separates private desire from public space; "Street", reproduced on the cover, does the same. They show him as fractured realist, not fantasist, and they question the rules of representation. The poems do not mention and the book does not include Grosz's fascination with the mechanical. His wedding portrait of himself and Eva shows her, curvaceous in pornographically flimsy shreds, and himself, as an automaton. The chosen tone the poet has given to Eva distances her from such erotic danger; she identifies with the anonymous respectable figures and with observers: "We are those passers-by. We have to keep walking." ("1918: 'What earthly good is art'", 24) and

> I keep quiet, let the idea of people and places
> paint themselves in ochre, a mass of swords,
> skulls, beer, brains and burnt-out doorways. ("Oil Painting: 1925", 38)

The virtue of this book is in this quiet, un-Grosz-like fidelity: to the paintings that Abegail Morley has chosen to include, to history. The poems are chronologically ordered; they show Grosz's contempt for his society from the Great War period, and then how it is gradually invaded by the rise of Nazism, and bring the story up to the couple's decision to emigrate. The chronology at the end records Grosz's later life, an underpaid art teacher, depressed, whose work had gone out of fashion, who died soon after his return to Berlin at the end of the 1950s. Morley starts a real conversation, both with George and Eva, she points us to the artist's work, and communicates how a passionate anger expressed in art can live on, can ignite new passions and new works of art.

The two books I've discussed make their entry quietly enough. Frank Osen's collection *Virtue, Big as Sin* (his first, at the age of fifty-eight) comes surrounded by big claims, a prize awarded by his publisher and an afterword and numerous endorsements from fellow-poets. The title refers to a Tiepolo allegory (though it's almost incidental to the poem in which the phrase occurs, "Portrait of Alexis Piron (?)", 9), and Osen appears drawn to certain forms almost as tradition-bound as the allegorical convention. The voices that echo here cultivate literary elegance; they include Wallace Stevens and Edwin Arlington Robinson as ancestors, but verse in rhyme and metre is alive and well in the English-speaking world. Among Osen's poems there are sonnets and that

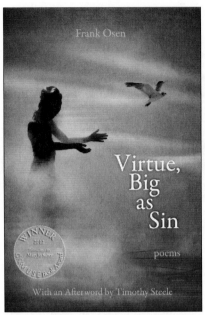

more intricate form cultivated by poetry-writing courses, the pantoum. This reader's eye slides over the technical showing off, preferring the quiet surprise and satisfaction when I discover that a poem about raiding his dead mother's medicine cabinet, ("Medicine Cabinet", 8) is also a sonnet. The great danger of rhyming poetry, the helterskelter *accelerando* stumbling over monosyllables, is not always avoided, and there is even an inversion-for-rhyme which hasn't been permissible, even in a brief and fairly witty poem ("Tell", 20), for more than a century.

The best of the poems in *Virtue, Big as Sin* are humane, interesting, serious, and they manage a clarity that comes from those qualities. Ballasted by a real subject – not infrequently family relations, death or danger – they can articulate the obvious in words that are given their impact by a context: the dead parent in "Pacific Drift" (6-7) for example, or a young person's funeral in "We Go Without You":

> The lesson here is one we've always known:
> you can be sheltered, loved, behave, do well,
> and half a breath may blow it all to hell.
> It's news we bury till the kids are grown. (59)

Some of the rhyming jokes are really good; there's a relish to "harpies" rhymed with "car-keys" in "Unawares, by Parrots" (50). Some poems are make-weights and wouldn't be missed. But among the limper parodies and the insightful comedy, and between the echoes of influential voices, Frank Osen's own poetic voice is strong and bears listening to. I will be interested to see what he does next.

Noel King experiments with many voices, making his second collection *The Stern Wave* a sort of sampler. Not all of his personae speak for themselves, and among the monologues some are solipsistic while others describe relationships, often intergenerational. A child knows too much about the reasons for her father's absence, a son worries about his frail mother. These voices and the poems where they are heard appear to me to be more successful than the pieces where he branches out and allows himself to speak for more exotic but also victimised figures. A child is taken from her family and trafficked for sex "though my bosoms still aren't there yet" ("Taken", 18), a boy in Trinidad learns to walk on stilts in a charitable drug-diversion project:

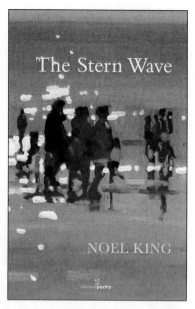

Steady, that what 'tis all about yo man,
in your country you fall off fuckin bicycles' – HIH HIH!
("Stilt School", 64-65; 64)

These speakers appear to me to have been saddled with an artificial idiom, made to sound awkward because they are young and unfortunate. In other poems the title tells us what to expect: "Drunk's Wife" (49), "Ordination Day" (40) – the priest's child is born and disposed of in a bog on the day of his ordination – "Aunt Jane was a fallen woman, my family said" (39). A poem less immediately placed, and to me more interesting, is "Guns", where a couple of middle-aged sons go shopping with their father, who

> chooses
> a Dickson Round Action, Side by Side, 12 grammes too.
> I see him seem to polish it with his left hand,
> his strong hands like mine, just older.

– and the (more than) slightly odd feeling of a children's treat prolonged into adulthood, and involving instruments of death, persists in the long last line:

> we'll shoot together, all three, every Sunday, we promise Dad that.
("Guns", 20)

A tense, calm piece like "Guns" suggests that Noel King is capable of writing more unpredictable, more restrained and skilful poems than the majority of those in this collection. He can be lyrical, as in "Where I Come From" (55) and suggestive, as in "Exposé" (59). He should allow these gifts to emerge. And his publishers should be more careful with their copy-editing.

Mary O'Gorman's *Flames of Light* is an attractive small book, celebrating memories, gardens, relationships and friendships. The title may sound like tautology but there is indeed something luminous about her writing, not only in her populations of blue rock thrushes, "glorious" narcissi and shining angels, but in the sharpness of her glance. Like Harry Clarke, a detail from whose stained-glass "The Vision" glows on the cover, she knows how the effect of brilliant colour is set off by dark lines. She can make a negative set off a longing, as in the final poem in the collection, ("I Can Move Stars", 52):

> … no words blend to cause
> your car to career up my drive
> and you to emerge, with bluebells
> drenched with Kerry rain.

Her unpretentious style can juxtapose family losses and personal adventures; poems set in Morocco or Zimbabwe are photographic stills which capture an instant of peace, or a shock:

> a dog waits near its dead owner
> who was knifed for the way he voted ("Zimbabwe, 2012", 35)

The achievement of this poet is that she convinces the reader that she is seeing what she describes so simply. Her voice is intimate, immediate and definitely her own.

Chapman's Homer

Taking a big breath
before swinging his fourteeners
the boisterous word-jammer
cursed those dry scholars
scared out of their wits

as Helen flouts Venus
shouting 'Cool your heat sky-queen
forget shape-shifter Zeus
bed pretty boy Paris
give me Menelaus'.

The daughter of Oris
high priest of Isis
was his tender wet-nurse
her long breasts
oozing honey

till the Sibyl's shrill frenzy
screamed in his skull
'Away with your lullays
build a tall temple
to all Makers and Muses'.

Blind but only an idiot
says he was born blind
no-brainer just see it
glint of javelin and helmet
ruined eyes jaws and gut.

He netted nine ring-doves
to flutter his nursery
raising the rooftops
with their cooing and calling
patter and brawling

while dulcet or raucous
he sang high and low
concerto of nightingale
missel-thrush partridge
blackbird and quail.

The cold shadow-master
praising and anointing
those he fears as divine
expelled him as alien
in Reason's republic

Paemius
his teacher
and think of it
Plato
Socrates his scholar.

DANIEL HARDISTY

Metro

Pelaw, Fellgate, Brockley Whins, East Boldon:
the suburbs have given way to flatness
and forgotten bales turning grey in fields;
the hiss-hiss and jerk of the Metro doors
and the pitch-shifting tannoy announcements
recorded far from here. Beneath a sign
which reads *priority seats* an out-patient
picks at his dressing, while a girl fishes
false eyelashes from behind her phone case
and in the black glass fixes them in place.
No one is watching, and no one is listening.
A few horses, grey as the rained-on hay,
refuse all interest in the passing world;
the corridor stamped with light which passes.

the owl man

his pockets full of dead mice
the owl man haunts the darkness

and why would he not?
he likes the silence
his pupils are dilated
his fingers grow feathers

silent shadows sweep
about him and
about his offerings
like agitated thoughts

they're friendly enough
he whispers *once they've
become accustomed to you*

and *they'll eat each
other's young* he adds
as though it were a good idea

his is an oilskin world
pulled inside out
darkness in light
light in darkness

stretching his arm into
a branch from which
small white furry fruit
hang stiffly until
every last one
is plucked

Wallet

She did not remember where she'd dropped her wallet
and discovered she had lost herself,

but, then, she was forever shedding things:
flats, friends, lovers. She was (I always felt) deciduous

and decidedly so. Now, returning to the empty
forest she retraced her steps, although there was little there

to find except turning leaves soon to drop and gather
and the detritus of a world she no longer had purchase on:

yellowing paper, crumpled cans, a lost left shoe (pink)
and a moon she'd never noticed, white between the branches.

But no wallet, though it was probably there somewhere in the shadows
of the tall trunks, along with her few banknotes, her cards, herself.

Route 1003

When the driver remarked
that he was a man of compassion
I decided that his was the best bus.

I liked the way he grasped the wheel
with a measure of insouciance
that belied his words

for he let the bus run idle
until I had aged sufficiently
to make the journey

and he seemed to know the time,
the exact time, for he eased out
into the traffic with a casual

[118]

wave to the road as if wishing
it farewell and banks of cars
parted like the Red Sea,

parted in acceptance of
his compassionate presence.

And comforted by signs such as these,
I closed my eyes and wept.

J. STEPHEN RHODES

Thawing Pool
After the painting by Willard Metcalf

Setting your easel next to the stream, bundled
in fur coat and derby, you put the ice shelf
at the center, already too diaphanous to reflect
mountains still locked in snow. You softened

its edges, as if its crust had become
a cloud you could touch, something between winter
and spring, where water was the clear winner,
making off with each interlocking crystal.

Water, that fifth column, poured out from a secret
corner in the woods and ate into drifts, exposing
ochre banks, a revolution already started,
something from nothing, a rabbit from a hat.

Two Paintings

After seeing The Thinker: Portrait of Louis N. Kenton, *by Thomas Eakins in close proximity to* Mr. and Mrs. I. N. Phelps Stokes, *by John Singer Sargent, at the Metropolitan Museum of Art*

Both of them hold their coat lapels back.
Both stand. Both dominate their canvases.
Both sets of hips tilt, though Edith's cant
to her right where she grips a straw hat.

Two paintings away, Louis's waist
is loose like the watch chain on his vest front.
His knees look ready to buckle, lost
in baggy pants, while Edith's white skirt

suggests lawn tennis or a jaunt by the shore.
Louis's chin blends in with his tie and falls
into a Puritan collar, the one thing
keeping him erect, as if it's attached

to a post driven into the floor.
Edith wears the more manly tie,
its bow outdoing the pleated blouse,
announcing the rise of the new woman.

Her jaw dares the viewer. Her ruddy face
surrounds an almost cocky grin.
Hands in pockets, Louis's eyes take in
the floor, though more likely an unhappy

conundrum he has grappled with before
and which he no longer cares to conceal.
Both of them are bold in their own way,
unapologetically happy or glum,

dressed and painted as they chose.
Breaking out of their frames, could they speak
to each other: he of time's burnishments;
she of unstinting hope?

IAN SEED

Phantom Limbs

After Maurice Merleau-Ponty

Clouds wander like thinkers in midair, only
to reassemble, remote on the horizon. Our flesh
takes its place among arrangements of fields,
their colours and smells formed in our hearts.

We do not see from our bodies as from inside
a box. We pertain to the whole, we take our place
in the landscape, in the touching of the sleek and rough.
A finger on the rim of a glass makes a ring

reverberate in the air. At a certain time you recall
another time on another day. This will always
be true. We move towards a thing of which
in the end there is nothing to say. This wave

rises within us between the touched and the touching.
If we break a stone, we can feel its pieces, but once
a picture is torn, it no longer exists. Yet if I look
or remember long enough, a constellation emerges,

pregnant with texture. Though it will change or disappear,
its fragments remain to touch lightly. No need
to make believe. Understanding comes from lingering
on the edge of these fields. Emptiness is not nothing.

Greetings

His face meets mine on the shore, with its freeze
furled in a dream of a lake. He asks me
who I am. A child enters by a secret door,
light as a fable, no longer wearing his coat.

A world has gone from his eyes. I picture
the house from outside, its stones the colour
of time. Ghosts are for the living. They nestle
and warm us at the stem. Nothing so still

as he who moves the past around in pictures
though it keeps running away. When we move
our eyes, the view changes: the distance comes
closer. The landscape and our wandering gaze

are glued together in the upsurge of a true
and exact world. Your finger plays across
its surface, pointing to a tree on the far side.
Leafless, motionless, it might be dead or alive.

And here's the slope going down to the water,
where an empty boat trapped in the ice awaits
with wordless logic. By the tree whose roots
are drowning, your hand stretches out to help me in.

Fidelities

The dark thing that lies upstairs takes
nothing for granted. It remains faithful
in a world of deserters, plotters and perpetual
beginners. Its footnotes alone have validity

at the bottom of a narrative coloured with fire.
The sun grows as it goes down. See that redhead?
I lace my shoes and cross the road, a stranger
but not of foreign blood. Is it okay to share

your toothbrush? Or to wear your pyjamas?
My dreams wander around the distant town.
One path makes me think of another where
flowers crowd or fall about you. Faces

[122]

vanish down the street. Some coatless exile
descends at the end of a station platform. The charms
of roaming through smoke where memory dirties
its own threads! In this clump of survivors,

we sift through pieces of each other's dreams,
fluctuating life stories to be shared, you
in his room on the bed, fast and slippery and wet,
a dark space between the real and not-real.

JOHN SIBLEY WILLIAMS

First Impressions of the City from a Broken Émigré

An impossible latticework of sky
hovers unreachable between impossible pillars,
domed in lights to keep the stars at bay.

The green patches squared between roadways
are littered in familiar glass shards,
dead weeds and compensation.

The tree that climbed you out of a distant childhood
now bends sickly beneath the weather patterns
born of concrete and neon ascension.

And in all your fallenness, still a husk inside stands upright –
broken and healed and ready
for a new kind of music.

Notes from a Cemetery

A perfect slice of sun pierces the gray above,
coming to rest on a headstone time-scoured of its name.

In time, smooth surfaces will define who we once were.
Eventually, I must try to become as smooth and unyielding.

       *

History has never been for the faint of heart.
Nor has sudden and unexplained light.
When someone else's life comes into my hands
I look to the past for answers
and repeat the mistakes I was raised on.

       *

Ivy grows thick as my grandfather's arm,
which I'm told once held things
like rifles and rail spikes.
A dead brick surface peers out from
the living gaps between us.
Still I shine like an infant about to be held.
About to, and never.

Beside me, a cradle rests on freshly-dug earth,
rocking back and forth over the stranger
who gave me these eyes.

       *

We all have reasons for wanting to be less,
for sitting alone in the shadow of our parents
and envying the silence that endures.

But I'm not yet as strong as the empty field
that stretches beyond the last gray cross,
where the gravediggers laid down their shovels
and remembered that not everything can be interred.

I may never be as strong as the field where nothing grows,
where the shovels that must come
skim across the surface
and splinter into a thousand pieces –
wood and iron.

Rooms with a View

The clockmaker lies on a bed,
surrounded by time
in various broken states,
and thinks of what he might see
if he looked out the window.

Like an animal becoming human,
the city pulses red below its skin,
rises from bone into self-reflection,
and thinks of what it might see
through the eyes of a man
who looks elsewhere.

Their days are spent
tinkering with springs
that continue to uncoil,
winding hands forward and back,
moving people closer to understanding
that they move ever closer.

And it makes no difference that there's a woman
across the alley, wearing a necklace
that might be the sun,
rising and setting with each heavy breath –
how she remains at the open window all day and night
in various broken states
and thinks of what she might see
if she closed her eyes.

A Kind of Intimacy

After Mark S. R. Struzan

We arrive nearly invisible,
despite our wailing,
into a world of forms.
We fail the promise
of making more from them than silhouette.
We fail the road. The breath in our lungs.

But we have a kind of certainty:
as we drop, the air parts around us
and reunites in our wake.
The earth accepts the weight we carry
and hollows out a place for us.

At first, everything is huge and closer than touch.
Unfamiliar, the sky in our eyes. We will fail that sky.
Like a paper mobile left turning too long,
distance unfolds gradually,
time doubles, triples, and before morning comes
with its unflinching parade
we have learned to stop wailing altogether.

But the air continues to part, temporarily.
The earth still burrows and smiles.
It is only the mind that struggles against
the body's indefinite shape, some distance away.

The Countries We Live In

They wash with sand where there is no water,
where the rivers drown like bodies in themselves,

and where we live, just south of any compass,
we scrub our tired hands with ice,
though we're surrounded by oceans
and bodies, beneath.

[126]

*

Some boy by the rail tracks
who sits like his dead father and worries
what kind of metal will next fall from the sky

runs his empty hands along the warming steel,
with its promise of progress, and hopes
that is enough to summon rainclouds instead.

*

Through shelled-out windows,
an entire town that shares one face
looks out upon what has become of home

and weeps like broken stars,
weeps for a childhood that cannot linger,
weeps for the dogs running mad through the streets,
becoming human.

*

My grandparents, cousins, and the siblings I've never had
gather for Sunday dinner, secure in the television's glow:

what is missing are the bones
from the meat we've raised and named
and slaughtered and praised,
like belief,

what is missing is the taste
of the apples sliced for our bread,

what is missing is what has always been missing,

and the weatherman warns us
just outside the windows we won't open
there are storm clouds stretching, unbroken,
over both horizons.

Cock and Pullet

I've got to tell you again: the sign outside Vander read: "For Sale: One Cock and Pullet."

Isn't "pullet" a wonderful word? Long time ago in the precinct of instinct I got the pullet's feet to eat. The bones were soft and yellow. I got also the neck, feet, gizzard, liver – giblets. The "best" parts interested my family: breast, drumsticks, thighs. My mother's favorite? She'd just wallow in the luminescence of the back. The lights in the lungs and the curds near the tail, plus that v-shaped rear I never ate, though I heard a grill-man say: "Man, that tidbit's the prize after the bird's done." He plopped it into a theatre eternity cannot imitate, his lips soused with Schlitz.

Little Jimmy Dickens loved to say he was so scrawny, because he always got the north-end of a chicken flying south. "That's why I look so bad and have such puny ways", he'd say.

Access to language gets sappy. There are more trees to climb. Words go astray on leaves to celebrate the Wrecks We Are. Whose fault is that? Is the crow of cock the yodeling doodle? How about the male fowl? We don't have woodcocks in our woods. If we did, plentifully, I mean, they'd be called "Cocks". I'll bet the cluck-bird in Chaucer's time made a sound like that – a cock-crow. Weather vanes are for the birds. I've seen photos of cocks drowned on steeples.

Cock-fighting's popular in some places, though legality's still the leg up.

I've never been the Cock of My Walk, though at times the strut gauges my constitution.

With fists I was never the Cock. I hated boxing, though one time Daddy got us some boxing-gloves from Sears. I can see the scrap of blood on the glove Brown hit me with. During this time he wanted to be a Charles Atlas. We never thought that might be a made-up name. Brown ordered The Charles Atlas Course. Substitute Angelo Siciliano and you see what I mean. That's wonderful – not to get your thoughts burned!

Believe in your heart. Let others break the news not worth Truth except the one knowledge lights in speech persuasion brings out at the top like stems on honeysucklebushes.

On the farm here at Paul's Hill I used to hear: "Cock the spout, Son, so the gas will go in the can." Little Roy Lewis was cocky the night he said, pooching his lips into the microphone: "I kissed my girl-friend good night – not one of these pecks on the cheek – it was a deep sucking kiss and she asked me – Where did you learn to kiss like that? – you know what I told her?" Audience: "Whaaaaaaatt – howwwwwwwwwwwwww?" Little Roy: "Siphoning gaaaas!"

My 12-gauge Iver-Johnson, single-barrel-squirrel gun, full choke, Uncle Reuben lent me $16.00 to buy, at Farmer's Hardware, Smithfield, NC, when I was sixteen (1954). I'd cock the hammer back all the way and shoot number-6 shot at a squirrel; boy, he'd fall and I'd feel proud to feel the warmth in my hunting jacket as I walked the wood-path home. Mama would fry my kill and I would eat the brains, cracking the skull with a knife to get that good stuff. Those days, no longer solvent, wave possibilities of wildness in a tomato patch ransacked with scallions. My mother, the gardener, kept her garden clean. I loved to help her do that.

My father always wore his Stetson when he went to the courthouse. He'd cock it, too, the way Whitman poses in that famous photograph. Daddy would cock his eye. You'd think he really knew something.

I don't see the cockaded woodpecker here on Paul's Hill. I saw a few in Weymouth Woods in the Sandhills, among the virgin long-leaf pines near Southern Pines.

I could go on rumbling out of road, looking for a cock and bull story. I feel like a cocklebur.

[129]

Anna Wooten used to see cockroaches under her toaster. Everything in the world's got to have a home. The boll weevil certainly proved that.

Life gets pretty low-down at times. I'm not cocksure of anything. The solid cast trashes burdens and chunks meanings. Let Cock Robin alone!

Collard Culture

Strike the cutting board for collards – not baggage –
Though a collard might not heart like cabbage.

You boil the water with a piece of salt-pork
Until the meat is tender – then take it out.

Wash the collards in cold water; they'll perk up and lounge.
Then wash twice in warm water to dampen them down.

Put them in a pan on the sink,
Twisting them with your hands and think

You want to lessen their bluster more,
Humming a song for someone you adore.

Cook the collards long as you wish;
Then use a spoon with openings – swish

As you become Supreme Drainer
Of liquor distilled from collards through a strainer.

Thoroughly pour them out – the whole lot –
Into a bowl and put the liquor in a pot.

You can drink the liquid – be sure you thicken
It with Mama's Homemade Crumbled-up Biscuit.

Your collards will give you heart
And cabbage won't cross your mind or part

Your taste for collards time and again.
The salt-pork's good to eat, too, settles the brain.

Why you'll fly out of the house into your yard
And coo like the collared turtle-dove-bard

And fight like the collared knights of old
During light and woo your Beloved – nights – hold

Her – your velvet-collar around your neck,
Your lover fitting her cheek next

To yours, snuggling close her collarette –
Making you desire collards for breakfast

Instead of the usual Food Lion Raisin Bran
Steeped in store-shelved raisins which taste like sand.

Mid-mornings you'll sense divine sanctions
All because a popular green vegetable's really rank

With culture forever distinct –
Why every farmer and his wife tend

A collard patch in the South –
Children – hush your mouth!

In winter cover the leaves with dirt –
(Protection from the cold) and strike the hurt

And cry No more boring stores and bother
For your every Calling will be *Collards*.

Chocolate Pecan Pie

I must stand in Mama's kitchen again
By the lonely array of eyes
And all I ask is that the ghosts
Come close to shape my memory
So that she comes back to manage the range
And smell up the room with fried chicken,
And some gravy and that special sweet-tea,
The chocolate pies, home-fries, and turnip greens.
I want the small game filling the house with howls
Of pleasure for being killed for our table.
Her stove-eyes bleed with imagined grace –
No surrogate's charge or substitute's rage,

For the Imagination of Shub's life reliving hers,
His perception a boost to her plenty
As she moves the year round her real motions,
Accepting her husband's humor that she was a Johnson;
Therefore she never looked where she was going.
In spring when the tobacco-plants embedded grew
She prepared her garden to judge the frost:
The peas, corn (roasting ears) clad in silks,
The butter-beans, snap-beans, and okra.
In summer when the sun showed slow rays
She'd don her bonnet to look like Granny (I told her to) –
The Granny of The Beverly Hillbillies.
The fall let her keep herself the same
Except she varied her life and work to the weather,
The October child she was – like her husband too,
Complete gold together as she got up before light
To pick cotton and then the dried September peas
While he got up the corn and put it in the barn.
The winter spared their lives in the plankhouse,
Especially at nights as they slept under several quilts,
The living room caught in restoration now
As I remember my father saying, "Here's where we slept –
In this room where cracks in the walls were so wide
You could throw a five-pound possum through."

My head gets swimmy with fishes she's fried,
Squash she's rolled in flour, okra she's stewed,
The rest, too, imaginable as a blank address her ghost
So beautiful and adorable, dresses rarely, forever.

And just to think, she'd turn from frying perch or squirrel,
Or barbequing possum or pork
To ask me what I'd like for dessert.
I'd say, "Mama, a Chocolate Pecan Pie, please" –
And it would appear – just like that –
Out of her Recipe Box of the Tacking Eagle:

> *1 unbaked pie shell*
> *1 stick butter*
> *2 ounces semi-sweet chocolate*
> *1 cup sugar*
> *2 eggs*
> *1 tablespoon vanilla*
> *1 cup pecans*

> *Melt butter and chocolate together over boiling water and mix with other*
> *ingredients*
> *Pour into pie shell*
> *Bake at 350 degrees 25 minutes*
> *Serve with whipped cream*

A woman emerges in front of a Home Comfort Range.
I am born in the moment, filling the reservoir
With water and adding stove-wood
I've toted to the wood-box.
Together we grow, without saying much,
Like "I love you" – though the words
Are always there, silent, rare,
So close we never make a point.

ROGER DESY

old news[*]

— flying south to the wetlands of their winter grounds

— resting on their migration route five million snow geese
burden and overstress thinning mid-west grain fields

no more than any other species takes control and owns
whatever paradigm will give it room and time to live and die

— stirring survival from oblivion neck muscles of stragglers

bending to peck the snow to sample grit and baubles
of waste grain will spasm in an early blizzard like any other

— caretakers — were ever there were any — need take care
they do not trample on the stillness of the fields they trespass

— since it is the fields that watch them — day and night —

with an equanimity that absorbs the fanatic echoing report

of a million spent cartridges striking a hard and bitter ground
with the twenty-percent no-limit harvest thudding the silence

[*] Some years ago a small item in the *Pittsburgh Press* covered this periodic
Midwest culling of snow geese.

movement

under plains of the moon they lie out there shadowed in bedded fields

– stirring on snow – stiller it is – the more they seem to stir –

trespassing grass nuzzling the naked tips – their ears against their necks
bent bristling between the inference of movement and the certainty of it

– surrounded by a studded dark the same dark distant as on snow
imprinted in the clefts of definition – breathing the frigid scent of clearings

– flaring – they exhale coils into the torpor of a quiet night that pulses
to the roots where little more than nothing may be all there is it is

– lured to remaining windfall – scraping soft depths to hardened ground

– transfixed on isolation they stand a moment in the middle of nowhere

till bedding down – attending the intensity in the surrounding stillness

only to rise again – nightlong all night they browse perimeters of fields

until the night and moon are gone beyond the whitening range reddening
behind a flush of squalls driving the surfaces of dawn – and then move on

natural

– their population browsing overpowers the buds and bark
of hibernating saplings – they do of course cause damage

– however never the destruction of their environment

no matter how bitter the winter – never the roots of grass –

the fields erupt again in spring – the incidental damage
decays to nutrients that germinate renewal into new growth

– injuries grow their scars and heal – as latent second buds
under the tips of spurs nipped off to satisfy survival

fill in the space filled out to full leaf in the sun – nothing

is missing – nothing taken – and though their own survival at times
forecasts starvation – satiety even in famine is given back

into the selflessness of the humility it came from – it's rare

almost unnatural – to find even debris of their remains in woods

– more than unnatural that the ground they trespassed – grazed
to its exhaustion – blow stubble of spent furrows into windy dust

loss

gazing into a blinding lucid shine

into the air into a stir of terns
making their way across the surface shoals

out to the breadth and depth diminishing
each wing beat to a point of blur faceting

an undefinable horizon – taking

the reach of eyes to the exquisite edge

– into the sun into the ice of light

try as one can to sift what interference
accumulates on outer distances

the retina of memory irritated
by the excited glare only retains

that scintillant erratic image burnt

by a bird lost – staring at clarity

MICHAEL PRIOR

Mary Writes a Letter
After *Clearing the Battlefields in Flanders*, 1921, oil on canvas

Dear Sir,

Here is my body, 46 years of age – already a canvas filled.
Enclosed is painting number 299 of 300 I will complete.
Sir, I am an amputee: a brush for a hand, an easel for a spine,
these are the transformations of the mud, the cold,
the things to which I am witness.
Sir, can you feel the iron in your bones,
the shift of the pigments in your face?
Here is my dream: a bayonet blossoms
from the ground like a flower, a crater
opens its mouth to swallow the stagnant pools,
the deepening geography beckons me
homewards like every lost friend.
And I, sir, capture it all.

Mary in Bedlam
After Jacob Polley

Cloudless chance has let it hang for half an hour inside,
her brain's a shuttered window, cracking with the cold,
the surfeit sense that what she owed was always by her side.
The faces she sees are homunculi, hiding in corners, attics, the old

friends she has to learn again, silhouettes crossing the sill.
And cloudless chance has let it hang for half an hour inside,
that shapeless stain upon her mind, the rust of synaptic will,
the surfeit sense that what she owed was always by her side

until now: the long slog over the fields of shattered Atlantic floes
with the friends she has to learn again, silhouettes crossing the sill
of her cabin in the evening, while the boat lurches over the icy shoals.
They whisper to those who will listen that Mary's mind has fallen ill.

Mary among the Wounded

The maple in the garden back home
has fallen, my husband writes. *A violent squall*
undid it all and tore it from the soil.

Its roots, he says, *were larger than all the branches*
we ever saw, and perhaps it's the same
with these poor boys:

                    although sight-shorn, shredded,
wet, and lonely within their pools of pain
there is some greater tree beneath them
                    we have yet to see.

They're delicate mannequins
to my eyes – porcelain features
defaced with chlorine, a chemical blade
they swallowed whole and couldn't withdraw.

There are thunderstorms here every night
like vast metal sieves sifting memories
from their minds. My role is to paint
what they would have seen
so that if they recover they won't be blind.

Note: These poems examine the life of one of the first female war artists, the Canadian painter Mary Riter Hamilton (1873-1954).

Hilda Sheehan

From "Frances and Martine"

The Dog

I caught a dog today, said Frances to Martine. A dog! Where did you put it? Now that is a question that would take all day. And they thought better of it. Frances made tea. Martine tidied-up her many dresses. But it is all. They did not discuss the caught dog or where Frances put it. They had all day. They were not in a hurry, yet. Not until the dog. They knew it meant the best not to name the dog (that nowhere was). Should they change their life on account of a dog? Where did Frances put it? But Martine could not stare at this question. Foolish to be so occasional and obsessed, no matter! Easy to just store a dog one day and let it go another. The dog did well to be so occasionally stored. Martine just about became able to separate Frances and the dog. Bark, she said. Show yourself! Frances perfectly fulfilled her letting go. Never not anyone saw this dog. And it never became. They thought better of it. Martine invented places of dog in weeks of car rides to Walmart. I want my misery back, behaved Frances. The dog would never believe you, frankly.

The Dream

Frances awoke with the fragments of a dream. Over breakfast she recounted how, when making love, she was an actual mouse and Martine was a lion and Frances, her love sounds were like roars and Martine's were tiny squeaks but Frances could not remember either of their lovers, only their love sounds: one hooted, one nothing but a lot of flapping, and Martine dismissed the whole thing as ridiculous, how could Frances know, and why would her mind make pictures like this during sleep with such a messed up sound track.

The Scars

Having written the whole of her head Frances undid her buttons and showed Martine the scars. I forgot to write about these, said Frances, unbuttoning more buttons and revealing more scars that Martine had never noticed even though they had walked naked together in this apartment for many years. Will you have them removed along with that tattoo or will you write about them so they can be seen by everyone who reads your poetry? Why would anyone want to see my scars Martine? You are only just noticing them today and I had to point them out. They are not a metaphor for anything I have been through. I shall button up, wait five seconds, then get changed into something red with a zip.

The Menopause

Have you ever done the menopause? Frances is doing the menopause, today, she is slowly turning into an old lady. Look at her skirt! It pirouettes in clouds of disappearing oestrogen as she makes one last dash into her peri-menopausal sports car to shop for her very last moon. Martine did the menopause with her mother, who died, crushed by falling wombs and heart-felt diseases passed on by generations of menopausers. Martine steers clear of Frances, her brown-drape mood swings from the 1970s take her back to her poor mother. Frances has friends who did the menopause some years earlier. They are glad she is actually trying it out: The menopause is good for you, they suggest. Toss men away in a bloodless rage that goes on for weeks. Let's have a party, raise high your dry vaginas, menopausers! Rub them in water-based childhood sweethearts! Cover them in dark tan tights! No knickers! Knickers are the prison of the vagina! Back from the supermarket, Frances opts for a lonely scan on her laptop, where all her internal errors are smear-tested on Facebook updates then tweeted. Retweeted@Frances, favourited: today I will do the menopause.

Little Fires

At least once a week
when the moon and planets
         come correct,

I light little fires for the Spirit
      that moves me far less often
      than the One I once possessed.

I gaze into compact flames
        & get undressed,
      manifesting elation & distress

as I paint myself a fresh
      soul of hot wax, cobalt blue
        & warm ashes.

Opening Day

Under a rusting sky
sinewy cranes of Baltimore
still pluck giant cubes
from well-laden guts
of high-hulled grey longboats.

Another frothy fishkill
too close to shore
shoves greasy tourists & even
hard crews away from harbor-park
into fevered stadia, rowhouse
dives, even up Federal Hill
for a peek through the cannon's eye.

On a dark artery they call Light
weathered men in grey jumpsuits
climb down slow into a fat &
sudden downtown sinkhole,
looking to patch a ruptured cloaca
& shore up our city of forgotten
homicides one more day.

Giotto's Circle
Diana Brodie

Giotto's Circle
Diana Brodie

Poetry Salzburg

"Diana Brodie's poems are haunted by deaths, losses and moments of shock followed by years of stoical acceptance in which the shock takes shape. The moments are sharp and cumulative. Sometimes they impinge on histories beyond the personal, fitting into time's shadow, at other times they view human fate on a broader geographical map. The words are precise and full of irony. 'From the dark hall, we heard the clack / of plates being counted out. / Grandmother had already / put the finishing touches to lunch / and to daring new interpretations of happiness.' she writes in 'Counting the Change', that last line holding the balance between irony and pathos on a delicate knife-edge."

George Szirtes

August 2013. 96 pp. ISBN 978-3-901993-41-1
£10.50 (+ 2.00 p&p), €13.00 (+ 2.50 p&p), US$18.00 (+ 3.00 p&p)

Canticles

1. A Steinbeck Aha

Peering upward from the apogee
of infinite soaring mirrors
I watch you stray far off course.
Thus is produced an aha moment
as luck exits the equation.

You're exposed like a water lily
that floats on thick firmament.

I fix my focus on
your dusty gray work shirt
as you stoop to pull chickweed
from ever widening cracks
in the pavement.

A bitter wind whips waves –
the lights of Seaside
cauterize Monterey Bay.

2. Transmogrified

He was kept after school
due to acute insubordination.
He fought substantiation,
a train at the roundhouse
getting loaded with coal.

He weathered transmigration
across riven continents
to make a stand as a race
that in time gained ground.

He tossed formulas down
crevices of secret canyons,
learned his lessons
devoid of impressions.

In accordance his teacher
made him recite ABCs
backwards endlessly.

3. Hat Trick

My shoulders pressed firmly
against the back wall
of McFly's nightclub
on Saturday night.
Capitalist ESPN beams
Giants battling Dodgers.
Budweiser ubiquitous,
the assembly salubrious,
will reach fever pitch
once music commences.

Then a commercial:
the black bear
bounces a basketball
between its hind legs
like a Harlem Globetrotter.

The best mudder won
the Derby this afternoon.
Subway cars ramble,
rattle in my ears
like bulletproof cobras.

Wonderbird

Grappling with the first words of the universe
the uninitiated Wonderbird sheds his feathers,
falls like Icarus, tumbling head over heels,
with no rabbit hole escape – summersaults, dazzled
as he encounters on his woebegone journey a dense
viridian jungle that teems with prehistoric animals.

So goes the commencement of a transformation
that proceeds on cue substantially devoid of motion
as though a solid electrified wall has been built
between Wonderbird and his ultimate destination.

Dejectedly mired in the pit of sabertooths that is
abject loneliness, solitary like an emperor without
a home, Wonderbird is at a loss to describe anything,
absolutely speechless. Then he slouches, slumps, slides,
takes a ride all the way down the Big Dipper's handle.

Slipping off the tail end of the handle, he becomes
weightless, lost in unfamiliar open space. But then
the purple Wordbird swoops in from her star-studded
plateau, chirps wildly, grasps him in her beak, makes
a break for high heaven, kingdom come and beyond.

Poetry Salzburg Pamphlet Series 8

Mario Susko
The Final Take
May 2013. 40 pp. ISBN 978-3-901993-39-8
£5.00 (+ 1.00 p&p), €6.00 (+ 1.00 p&p), US$8.50 (+ 1.50 p&p)

"Susko is a metaphysical time keeper, a philosophical detective sifting through the desolate inconclusive evidence left by war and human desolation, the relentless alienist unraveling through dialogue and symbol, the deceptive tangle of memories and dreams, probing the borders between sanity and madness, reality and dream. He is a cinematographer of language, capturing the dialectics of existence and survival in flickering, indelible images."
Robert Karmon

MARK ROBINSON

The Working Writer

It's quiet. Too quiet.
There's a sentence out there
with my name on it.
It's been stalking me for days now,
through the murky shadows
of my working life, the talk,
the listening and the play-back,
the information and the deadlines,
the choices and the decisions,
the thought, the often apologising
and always explaining of my hours,
every casual word a message.
I've been breaking my own rules
and the sentence wants revenge.

It has secretly been in training.
It has been swimming rivers
in the cold of the morning.
It has sung blue curses to the mirror.
It has done push-ups and sit-ups
and now it is ready to run.
It wants to tell you all about me,
about its dismay and its dreams.
It lets me twitch under the quilt
while the garden tightens with frost.
It has made a list of all the things
I do that make it laugh.
Now is the time, it whisperingly warns,
for a line to be drawn.

Tradition, Traduction, and Truth

Mark Robinson. *How I Learned to Sing*. Middlesbrough: Smokestack Books, 2013. 202 pp. ISBN 978-09571722-6-5, £8.95 pb.

Fiona Sze-Lorrain. *My Funeral Gondola*. Honolulu, HI: Manoa Books / Berkeley, CA: El León Literary Arts, 2013. 59 pp. ISBN 978-0-98339198-2, US$18.00 pb.

Helen Ivory. *Waiting for Bluebeard*. Tarset: Bloodaxe, 2013. 112 pp. ISBN 978-1-85224-975-5, £9.95 pb.

Robert Sheppard. *A Translated Man*. Bristol: Shearsman, 2013. 130 pp. ISBN 978-1-84861-284-6, £9.95 pb.

With his influential magazine, *Scratch*, as well as his own poems, Mark Robinson was one of the original participants of the airbrushed Great Poetry Surge of the 1980s and 1990s (forget about the "New Generation" stuff – that was the metropolitan establishment waking up to what they'd failed to see and which they'd played no part in producing). When he progressed from vegetarian chef to arts administrator, turning from metaphorical poacher to gamekeeper, he took a decade-long, self-imposed sabbatical from publishing his work. For the poetry world this was a loss, but with this excellent collection from Smokestack Books we can catch up with what we missed.

"The world is a place that has changed and I need your help" ("Voice from the settee", 183) the poet says in one of his earliest pieces, and it could be taken as a primary motif of all his work. Robinson has become a chronicler not just of his personal life – marriage, children, getting older – but also of the society in which he lives. His world is a very local, rooted one (the north east), shaped by the

1980s and 90s, that is, by the great shock of Thatcherism. The early collections are accordingly oppositional.

"The Horse Burning Park" ("fun for all the family"), title poem of one of those earlier books, is reminiscent of the Northern Surrealism of Ian MacMillan and the late Martyn Wiley, nailing the dark comedy of an environment in which clapped-out industries are extinguished, only to be instantly revived as ghosts called "heritage":

> No, the horses were in actual fact
> burnt indoors, in 'burning sheds'.
> The Park is an attempt to capture
> the excitement without the grime. (178)

What is gone is gone and cannot return. There is a reluctance by some writers to come to terms with this fact, but it looks like Robinson, perhaps influenced by his spell on the other side of the funding fence, has seen the complexity of political decision-making at first hand and come to some sort of terms with it all. Those changes are not only irreversible, but they're now so far in the past that there are new generations who have no experience of them. It is telling that in finding a way to deal with this Robinson has inverted the high seriousness of Rilke's original *Duino Elegies* to produce a semi mock-heroic version of that new post-industrial world, culturally self-deprecating in a rather English way with its tentative hopes for the future. Some of the various angels of a now long-departed industrial base are glad that the actual misery of the romanticised past is gone:

> Old men on the surface trying on slacks,
> faces veined with years of black, delighted
> now the bastard pit is gone, built over.
>
> ("V. Dalton Park / Murton", 24)

There is a leaven of humour in much of Robinson's writing, however, some of it conveyed through experimentation, as he has always been open to varying the delivery, particularly when it comes to performance. Many of the pieces, e.g., "Domestic Comedy", rely on repetition as the driving principle:

> The real thing is the thing that is not there.
> As I walk in the room, my mother walks out.
> The real thing is the thing that is not there. (39)

[149]

Some of these have a rather Oulipo-ian feel, although the context of Robinson's work is quite different from that of Robert Sheppard, who also utilises similar techniques in *A Translated Man*. Although I find most of them entertaining, I don't think they're as convincing as the main body of Robinson's poems.

Still, that's a minor quibble about a solid collection of poems whose language is muscular and discursive, employing a very handy "pick it up and use it" method that allows the poet to accommodate the domestic, the political, the observational and the surreal. For me, though, the great strength of his work is the straightforward human warmth it demonstrates, particularly when directed at those closest to the poet himself. Many of the newer poems look backwards into the poet's past, particularly the lives of his parents; the title poem of the collection, "How I learned to sing" taking us right to the point as the poet remembers a family day at the coast:

> and now my voice has gone soft,
> crying for what I can't get [...]
> looking down on the strip of beach
> at the family I could not reach,
> and singing *back back back*. (45)

If you want to get the best of Robinson, I do not think you can do better than "My Love", which is one of the finest contemporary love poems I have read, and exactly as Milton said poetry should be, simple, sensuous and passionate – and economically short, deploying clear images, and a sure sense of rhythm and pace: "Such a long time ago now, and nothing to be done, / which is why I bring you fruit and drink and hope." (70)

As Pound wrote in Canto 81: "What thou lovest well remains, / the rest is dross"; and with this poet's talent and our luck what remains is a poem like that.

Fiona Sze-Lorrain's *My Funeral Gondola* operates in a different realm altogether, one that is defined by a cultural melding of east and west, and of music and language. Sze-Lorrain is a classically trained professional musician whose main instrument is the *zheng*, a form of Chinese zither, on which she plays both classical and modern music. She has performed in Europe and American and now lives in Paris. This helps account for the movement between the deployment of certain images, e.g., moon, clouds, flowers, etc., in a way we associate with traditional Chinese and Japanese poets, and the use of more modern and modernist approaches – prose poems, anecdotes and the occasionally Eliotic exercise. Her versatility extends to prose poems, which, for me, vary in success. One of them, "Visitor", in which the poet thinks about her grandmother, successfully delivers a powerful examination of past and present: "How the past not mine comes back faster than old fears [...] After marrying a Communist she learned to be sparing with passion and images." (44)

"Diva" exemplifies the Eliotic approach, quietly poking fun at a singer whose talent and self-absorption are in an uneasy relationship with her personal, and it seems solitary, private life: "With an assassin's smile she waters her plants / while scratching her armpits." (11) The mole on her face is fake and she is given to drink: "Empty demijohn clasped in her bosom she hiccups / and sleepwalks down the corridor." (11)

The sharp observation and satirical edge of "Diva" is taken up again in "Digesting an Academic Symposium, Some Months Back" (52), in which the poet is as much a target as the others: "I was grateful / because I was invited" (53).

As the collection's title suggests, in its rather gothic way, the poems continually float through meditations of mortality, including the poet's own. The process throws up unexpected images, realisations and secrets. In "Francois Dead", for instance, the poet appears to be remembering helping Francois (or is it someone else?) tidying up his room, to discover a book of translations: "Francois said he stole it" (23). But how sure can we be what is happening here, given the tricksiness of the poet's account, when she says "He lights the lamp, we return to dust" (23), playing on the double meaning of "we turn to dust" to indicate our own inherent mortality?

Many of the pieces possess a surface attractiveness, without necessarily opening up to further understanding, but most of them are redeemed by a clarity of image and diction, especially when working in a contemporary or recent context. This happens in "My 1980", for instance, where the poet enumerates various items from her life: "John Lennon died. / I started to visit museums" (45) she says; but if you thought she was too serious a youngster she brings you up with "An interest in toilet bowls. And who sat on where." (45) Altogether the collection has enough charm and individuality of voice to draw you repeatedly back into it; and it is a beautiful piece of book production as well.

If Sze-Lorrain's poems seem to float just below the surface of consciousness in a somewhat fantastical zone, then Helen Ivory's plunge us into deeper and more disturbing regions. *Waiting for Bluebeard* presents a modern vision of Freud's Family Romance gone wrong, where the weak and repressed father of the narrator's childhood returns as the abusive husband in the figure of the violent, woman-destroying Bluebeard.

These are tightly controlled poems, astute in their choice of images, combining a psychological realism within folk and fairy-tale settings. The first section gradually grows from the self-absorbed environment of the child-like into the grown-up apprehension of the world, moving from immediate family to ancestors, grandmother and great grandparents, as the narrator struggles to establish an independent identity within a future, adult existence.

The poems are replete with the imagery of skin, of disappearances, of insubstantial, ghost-like identities – "My father was a shadow / who stood at the school gates" ("Night Shift", 51). At the heart of this tale is the failed marriage in which violence is never shown but often hinted at. Things are always being turned inside out or upside down; the toy house in "Playing House", is "an upside-down box" (19), for instance; there's "The Inside-out House" (74) with its "innards tumbled onto the grass", and a poem in which the narrator took her father's book, "turned it upside-down / and filled up the last pages" ("My Father's Accident", 52).

The second section, dealing with the Bluebeard figure re-enters the elemental, sinister folk-world of the earlier pieces, replete with wolves, birds, bones, skin, moons. Bluebeard, for all his violent oppressiveness, is himself a damaged creature who "sobs like a wolf / from his leather armchair." ("Bluebeard at Night", 98) In visiting his own despair on the narrator, though, he empties her out of her own identity, just as her distant mother and ineffectual father had done, destroying her sense of selfhood so that she is always in the process of disappearing: "And by teatime she couldn't recognise / a single hair on her head ("The Disappearing: 8", 106).

There are some outstanding poems in the collection (one of my favourites is the superbly accomplished "What the Stars Said" (21), in which the dissatisfied stars convince a child to let them stay under her bed, only to start burning holes in the rug). At the end of this saga, the narrator has escaped Bluebeard, achieved some sort of understanding of her past, but is nevertheless haunted by the father figure, whose love she cannot have ("Hide", 111). We are left wondering just what hopes or terrors reside in that father's "love" and how long it will continue to dog the narrator.

Robert Sheppard's *A Translated Man* plays a completely different game from the poets above, taking us into territory where we have few traditional bearings to guide us. As the blurb says, Sheppard has given the book over to the fictional translations of a fictional Belgian poet, Valckenborch who has conveniently vanished. We're already dealing with multiple refractions of identity and authenticity.

There is a great formal diversity to the collection accompanied by much fracturing of syntax, repetition, leaps of language and meaning, and restless movement across the page. The words are continually looking for spaces into which to rearrange and order themselves, one moment disposing themselves like good poems down the left-hand side of the page, at other times tabulating themselves in columns, at others leaving large gaps between lines and sometimes becoming prose.

Language here is being used to reveal itself as much as any "meaning" proposed by the poet; it's a continual playground of the erotic, the psychological and political, where whatever it is we conceive reality to be within a poem is subject to questioning. Even the choice of nationality poses questions of identity and authenticity: Belgium being a fissiparous place, split between cultures.

A couple of poems offer hints as to ways to understanding what is going on. "election day glance poems" (44-47), for instance, is prefaced with the formula:

form: glance
content: chance

to which the answer is – "response: dance" (44)

So for the reader the form or mode of operation is to glance at the world; the content is provided by chance (hence the frequent juxtaposition of disparate things), so don't always expect simplistic connections; and the best way to respond (both for the poem and the reader) is to dance. Just enjoy the play. Performing a kind of magic, in some ways. In this particular poem the playfulness comes in the form of a satirical poke at politicians and the political process:

message to all liberals *if*

you carry on putting crap
through my letterbox i'll
vote flaams belang (47)

The obsession with flags is ridiculed through the constant interpretation of their colours and the whole process is presented as a drab, dull, pointless exercise. You may, indeed, as the voice says earlier, end up having to "vote for yourself" (44).

"The Word" also provides a way of looking at this work. It starts with the simplicity of the word "Sky", then immediately gets taken over by the language machine of the imagination – "Sky the hue of a sick egg unbroken", after which we are taken through an examination

[154]

of the relationship between "reality" of objects and the "reality" of the poem as it employs language: "Smoke for blocked chimneys, shallows of blue / in the depths open up. Like the poem." (75) Take the poem on its own terms, then, as of equal reality as the material it appropriates and presents to us: "Anything that enters the sky is the sky. / Anything that enters the poem is the poem." (75)

It is not possible here to cover the vast range of Sheppard's output within this collection. The linguistic dexterity is impressive, the cultural allusions positively promiscuous. Numerous poets, writers, artists and musicians enter the poems (there's a brutally erotic re-working of Ovid, for example, and a poem on Kevin Ayers that reminds me of pieces in Barry MacSweeney's *Odes*). It's a challenge but anyone who can start a poem with "under a confection of fucked chandeliers" ("cow 1", 63) is definitely worth spending time with.

Poetry Salzburg Pamphlet Series 9

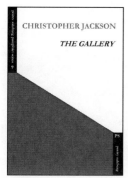

Christopher Jackson
The Gallery
September 2013. 44 pp. ISBN 978-3-901993-42-8
£5.50 (+ 1.00 p&p), €6.50 (+ 1.00 p&p), US$9.00 (+ 1.50 p&p)

"'We look back at our looking towards us.' This line catches the essence of *The Gallery* with its central conceit of being a guide to an exhibition of the poet's experiences (well sustained by evocative 'catalogue excerpts' between sections). Christopher Jackson's rich, dense poems include responses to music and artworks, locations as diverse as Brompton Cemetery and the African savannah and events such as the Occupy protests. Their sometimes dark tone is skilfully offset by bold, affirming images: 'the sky is a vineyard graped with stars'; 'the side of our theatre / is leopardy with leaf.'"

Mike Bartholomew-Biggs

CAROLYN JESS-COOKE

Planet

It is the tragedy of childhood that they do not
know how much I love them –
my shining boy with his four-year-old eagerness to make me proud,
my baby girl – plumpness, sunshine, all quest and zest,
my two year old – soft warm ivy around me at midnight,
a garden of language blooming daily in her mouth,
and my eldest – beautiful dance of sand and light, mirror
drinking all of me in and throwing all of me back.
They hear it daily, *I love you, I love you,*
they know my heart
has grown ears and eyes for them, has its own arms
to carry their hurts, would walk out of my own flesh for them.
But still, they do not know.
They have yet to find measure for this love, *genus, potestas,*
though they bathe in it, though it stretches over and under them
like a planet they tread upon, breathing its air,
sleeping all its trembling nights.

Baptism in Four Elements

I expected it to be like a cardigan of wind,
a liquid that was two parts Africa, nine parts me,
    itinerant nook, a kind of language I already spoke,

    and when they placed her on my belly, backwards,
immensity of blue noise, I felt halved – they don't tell you
    how pregnancy pushes your organs around,

    that you'll have to keep gathering them up in the sack
of your abdomen for a good week after, I kept pushing back
    curtains of fire, and when I embraced agony

flame became part of me, and when it did I thought
its waters could be sailed, sleep was a coded symphony,
   I couldn't feed her, despair was my skeletal cloud,

they said she was thriving, each morning fresh disbelief
that she was still here, my fears were half wind, half earth,
   I cleaved days of rock, so many of my faces rinsed off,

and when the human in her stirred, the creaturely body
unfurred, slowly I became it – robed in earth, wind-pearled,
   sea-stitched, forged in love's flame, I am more than

mother, more than sky – for her I am the fifth.

When a Girl Becomes a Mother

When a girl becomes a mother there is no fanfare.
No government re-elections, no erupting volcanoes.
The baby mops up the praise. But quietly
there are earthquakes and realigning planets.
When you ask to hold her newborn you are
addressing someone who just became a tiger,
so be careful. When she soothes the child that has
shrieked for three hours she is the Matador,
sunlit with relief. Sometimes, at around 2.47 am,
she is the only woman ever to have given birth.
At the supermarket she is a calm strong oak
dragging a thrashing child past the strawberries.
At the school gates she's autumn weeping leaves
of every hue for the loss of summer. Often
she spies the girl she once was and thinks, *wimp*.
Like grass trees after fire, like crops in new weather,
like a river clasping different water, there is
no fanfare when a girl becomes a mother.

A Kiln

A Neolithic kiln had been unearthed
one field away (the Stone Age is a field
away, in Orkney). It had been unearthed
and reconstructed here; remade to yield
new pottery to old designs rehearsed
five thousand years before: a new kiln filled
with heat approximating ancient fire
and soft clay, like a monster's fruitless pyre.

It was, apparently, a pile of earth
and mossy stones, dug open so a hole
containing pottery and smoky breath
lay in it like a pregnancy of soil-
smeared vessels slowly hardening in the mouth
of decombusting charcoal. Every coal
lit in there warmed clay cold for centuries
into a white hot flicker of degrees.

The pots which then emerged from it were small
and shattered easily, to ostraka
bespeaking exile from their actual
environment. They were like tesserae
in Gnosticism – broken by unreal
and unseen presences, before you have
one handed to you, proving that there is
someone behind you, hidden. Or there was.

And now, when I hold one smooth sherd in my
left hand, I am uncertain if what rolls
through my warm fingers is not certainty
negated, since it is a cold thing full
of strange mechanics, glazy sophistry
and silence. If it is an obol, cool
in Charon's hand, or silver sixpence for
Saint Peter, is, like Orkney light, unsure.

Dante's Last Prayer

Lord, if I am sent to heaven
let one or another of my eyes be sent to hell

beside a portion of my tongue.
Let it be the one

with which I first perceived the nipple
of a woman

not my mother
and that portion of my tongue

which was the first to taste an apple.
Let them be

put in the fire
among my enemies

and former lovers;
mocking some

and bringing me
the taste of others.

Beach Pebble

I have been listening to it now a year or longer,
pressing its cold greenness to my ear and listening hard
for what is going on inside. If there are angels dancing
in there, then I have not heard them, but suspect
they move too quietly for our human ears to catch
and, if they sing, have voices like the thoughts of birds –
are always moving, startled, further from where we
stand underneath them, silenced by their fleeting song.

WILLIAM GILSON

The News Is Not News, It's Next to Nothing
(Actually We Don't Know What Is Next, but Something Is)

When the arrow gets to the edge of time
it appears to swallow itself, the point
pushing back through its incoming length, then
it begins pulling that length thru all of its previous path.
We won't live to see the next reversal
at the distant opposite edge. We will by then be
dead as door nails.

The atoms that make up door nails are tiny spheres of motion;
you can't pin them down. You can pause them
only with your mind: *there's* one! But
that pause is imaginary, all it does is disrupt
other processes, such as
the spider's exactitude: the orb of the web comes out flawed.

Twist the pencil-thin plastic rod with a leftward turn,
open the slats of the blind.
Eastward beyond the roofs of Kirk Barrow, of Ghyllside playing field,
and the distant grey stubs of castle, a long segmented silver Pendolino
glides southward.
Here, just outside this window glass, a spider
has spun a single horizontal line from frame edge to brick corner.
Tip-toeing, it dabs to that line with its spinnerets
two further threads, converging them downward; and from where they join
spins a long single vertical, attaches it, tautens it.

I have difficulty in knowing what's going on.
Guesses, and memories of reading, vicarious pleasures
of the Maine woods, two white men and "The Indian",
whose name was Joe Polis. He and Henry Thoreau
raced down the path along the river, Polis
carrying on his back the bark canoe, Henry
carrying the pots and pans (which he dropped

[160]

and gathered again).
                                                "O, me love to
play sometimes", said Polis.

Is the song that Joe Polis sang in the tent before sleep a string,
leading to yet another universe?
Is it a melody that a man, such as myself, might travel down?
Might I meet, coming the other way, a
counter-melody: that bluegrass tune called "White Dove" that
I long ago sang in harmony (amazing myself) with the woman
whose name
I can't remember?
She sang it again, by herself at the funeral of our friend Eric.

From somewhere, from the disproven ether, the Indian calls:
You follow that string you go to other universe!
Or do I imagine his voice,
now as I move this pencil?
                                You come out different door!

Ah yes: I remember now: not the door to the crapper, the loo,
the bog.
Nor the Men's Room, the Ladies'.
Rather the one with the sign missing, where,
against my better judgement, I looked in the mirror.

Holy shit! I exclaimed.
Holy shite! I said,
What in the fuck happened to you?

Too late – the missile, it's launched. It's
almost out of the tube.
Rising, clearing the rim, for a half-second it seems ponderously to pause,
as if about to fall back.
But then quickly it settles into its roar.
Up it goes.
Picking up speed.
Still leaking fuel, still spewing vapors.
It singes my eyebrows, it sunburns my face,
it sings its big song.

[161]

Cloth Ears

The suicidal fall of tiny hairs
housed in the inner ear: traumatic or
age-related hearing loss. In his book
Deaf Sentence David Lodge, or his narrator,

a Professor of Linguistics, loses
his hearing, retires early. Students,
we read, can only concentrate on speech
for twenty minutes, unless that speech is broken

up with re-cap, discussion, impromptu Q
& A. Without his hearing our hero
cannot engage his students in spaces such
as a lecture hall. Susurration makes

speech a struggle in shiny hard-edged classrooms.
The squeal of background noise with
a hearing aid turned up tries the nerves.
There are looks, sniggers, non sequiturs.

Blindness in literature asserts itself
as tragic, Deafness as comic, claims Lodge.
Consider Church Beer. Sorry,
Shakespeare. (Lip-reading is difficult too.)

The blind are seers and oracles. The deaf
are dumb. Or we don't try hard enough.
Even amongst the liberal classes, impatience
is rife: 'Have You Got It In?' 'HAVE YOU

CHECKED THE BATTERIES?' Excuse my whine,
plastic is not perfect. To return to the book:
at a Christmas party our hero's wife
tells little Lena that Grandad is an Eeyore,

meaning grumpy. Later the Prof rifles through
his childhood copy of *Whinnie-the-Pooh*
to track the grey beast down. Is he really deaf?
There's Eeyore on his birthday, raising

a hoof to press his ear forwards,
wobbling on his three remaining legs.
'Look at Eeyore!' we laugh at the picture.
'Look! Poor Eeyore's deaf!'

Dull

In bed there is a sound of running water,
maybe drains, or water from the gutter,
I don't know which, there's something wrong with my ears.

Perhaps, the sound is from the bathroom: a tap left on?
My partner gestures to the window '… kale?'
But I didn't hear the gale last night

despite this constant whishing. Nor do I
get the central heating's tick, the gurgles from
our frost-free fridge. All background sound is gone –

it's something to do with pitch. I don't hear
my partner in the shower, the kettle boiling,
the car leaving. I worry

about taps left on. I miss birdsong.

Kevin Ducey

Cahokia

And the knives of this table
have wounded me all over my palate.

César Vallejo, "Trilce XXVIII"

Disturbed in slumber
the blue copper birdman
oxidized in a cobalt-spark
shower of archeologists:
                    the mid-century
diggers ruthless with the pickaxe,
toothbrush, backhoe: Robert
Benchley's granddaughter,
Elizabeth, ran a dig here in Central
Illinois and came up
all Santayana.
            Griffin
could appraise three hundred
pot sherds in an afternoon
faster and more accurately
than the cellular analysis
that finally replaced him.

Some of us did not miss
John Henry, his bullying –
sitting in front at the conferences,
scoffing, here's
a cup of dust to your health.

                No, he was an ass, yet –
                always some new Galileo
                instrument coming down the path
                says you had it wrong all along.

[164]

Following along the Texas coast route
(the escape path of DeSoto's crew),
the Huasteca used the Northern copper as
in the Yucatan
            the English
                  traded powder and
muskets for mahogany.
               The lieutenant
straight-backed in red tunic
listened to the Speaking Cross
at Chan Santa Cruz, at Bacalar
the voice came through
a long speaking tube,
while the Spanish listened
behind the walls at Campepepeche.

Hey, English, get us Texas,
and the oil at Tampipipico
and we have the Republic
of the Americas – with your
West Indies – the American Lake.

And Nelson Reed, the amateur with
a Mayan history digging in Illinois,
taking a road-grader to the top
of Monk's Mound
            removing
six inches of topsoil
              (and a good deal of sculpture).
The mound revealed:
            post-holes,
                building foundations –
all there. Not simply a pile of dirt
stuck in the path of the American
Interstate system and the struggle against –
well, whatever it was that tribe
struggled against.

[Though the violence Reed did then
to the site – in his zeal
to stay ahead of the paving crew –

The trade off: dig with the bulldozer today,
or wait for a finer tool – if
the thing will wait for you.]

It won't wait: Later the bankers and insurers
came through, and the student/diggers
no longer camped out in the mud
like their poorer brothers in DaNang. These
excavations now proceed by sonogram
not a stone disturbed as
the birdman and all his blue dolphins
watch from the trees.
                    That night in Bacalar
Lieutenant Blake observed
the Maya assemble before a house
in which the Speaking Cross
was kept, the guerrillas prayed and
made music until about eleven o'clock when
                                    the prisoners
were brought out – men, women, and children –
and forced to kneel in the street.
Over the children's crying, Blake heard
'the squeaking, whistling noise' of God's voice,
the holy of holies wanted four thousand pesos
in ransom for the prisoners.

Fifty young women,
possibly Wisconsin Oneota
(if such a tribe ever existed),
stupefied
with 'a good deal
of tobacco',
had their throats slit, then
were tossed into the burial pit –
no, tossed isn't it,

nothing is ever haphazard
in funerary placement –
they took their places
(as though the curtains were about
to rise on a single speaker) alongside the
blue copper birdman on the
headlands above the Middle Mississippi –
a short stretch of road down
from the dog tracks and beer joints
of East Saint Louis.

Refill, hon?

"They finally staunched the hemorrhage with
two long plastic tubes inserted into his nose
and inflated ..." I hung up the phone, making

my excuses. Went to laundry, then breakfast
at the Greek place. Wondering about the
Peloponnese that they so learned their way

about an egg. Reading another Vallejo
poem – awaiting a death of mystery and
the inexplicable opacity of a flesh-eating
bacteria at work in the lungs until one is made

to feel a sensation of drowning irrefutably
figured as the waiter arriving now with the urns
of her sacred office – turning the oval of my
cup dark, the shade once of the old man's eye.

Edge to Edge

Sentiment trashed –
matchless zero, days of terror.
Old magazines, forgotten, stacked,
and so much principled behavior –
organic fresh rosemary, cauliflower,
purslane in the salad.
Manifestos' brickbats.
Will make make enough moxie,
will fallen leaves, bared branches, shredded paper do?
Unleavened bread, foul breath, scraped off dirt, ...
list superceding list,
while overhead a dreamy kind of blue.
Ballyhooed movies flourish fists, lethal strikes, parted lips,
a trumpery of ruse and quicknesses,
in   validating yesterday's harshness,
yet, still, a scent of roses from a garden,
and in the distance
a couple waving goodbye to their daughter.
Small claims forfeited.
Everyone pronounced fit
as, surely, the most treasured drink rosewater.

A murmuring 'will be' stays.
Consonant with danger,
dogs dribbling at the edge,
the prayerful relent.
The surging waters beat.
Edge to edge people press
sanguine in their brief.
Mildewed canvas, clouds and fallen leaves,
rotting timber, tincture of ...,

tincture of belief.

Always distant footsteps.
Nondescript tappings

make me sit up.
Stainless steel sutures seal my chest.
Crushed apples underfoot.
No matter,
October rain,
spring mud,
hallway walls with darkened red, dried spots.

Way Out

Way out, past saving, deaf to shouting.
A sea wall holding,
blues in migration
flashing in a leftover light.
Will there be catamarans embarking?

Obsessed by tomorrow, an edgy today further narrows,
while yesterday swells into a hugely amorphous bindle,
farther than away, than outside of self
marginalized by vatic longings,
petty past piques, uncontrollable misinformation –
that it does not matter does not matter.

I am halt,
waste,
arbitrary state,
neither creditable
or liable.
I am a temporary fix.
What else could have been arrived at,
what jaundiced view could have prevailed?

Ah, intimate matters,
not scoffed at, balked over,
whether as small as minute,
or
topless
as last night's dancers.

Regarding Stones

The Place hath yet some Ruins to shew ...

Anthony à Wood: September 16th, 1657

some stones had survived:
a cloistered wall; a pair of
ornamented towers, the west window's
tracery rising above lanceted doors
obscuring the prospect
of a Cotswold hill

stones:
mossed, lichened, ivied –
homes to spiders, midges, flies,
time-arrested snails

after six centuries since their founding
on Benedictine silence, hardly classic
deconstruction, an Earl's men
hurling down the stones, hearing
the thudding of them on the ground

too much and too soon for
Thomas Barncote – most of his lifetime
he'd revered the stateliness of ruin –
such melancholy was in his delight

and hardly classic reconstruction –
an Earl selling the stones to build
a few new Eynsham houses

later, six cairns also built
to instruct the pilgrims – this they do
reverently, silently

London with the Parable of Dives and Lazarus

Acrylic on paper, Timothy Hyman R.A.

Doesn't matter how the city stacks up –
fragile banks; shrinking churches;
cleaving river, the random divides –
Dives will always be portrayed as
a city-rich with pocket, hearth
and belly satisfied

while every inclement night
a Lazarus will die crawling from
a city-rich's door – every night city-dogs
will come greedy for weeping sores.
Every night the mercy-dove will fly
its vital mission carrying a Lazarus
to the patriarch dawning in the sky.

But note the memento mori: the city,
at times, can get too hot for the city-rich
then there's a price to pay – a sacrifice to
the high-life to be made, their own fat
fuelling the fire. And with it comes
the plea – the promise that in future
any Lazarus will know fair-play

though that matters not: still too easy for
another of the brotherhood to ignore
a Lazarus knocking at their door.

TODD PORTNOWITZ

To Leopardi

You and your beloved hedge,
we, before the Hudson Palisades:
How much more infinite our infinity!

Hubble knows, it's still spilling its dark guts.
All the millennia it may take to get to Jersey,
Hoboken some potentially habitable exoplanet.

Try casting a thought beyond that bluff –
to send it by electric train
you'll have to dig through the turn of the century,

three decades in a riverbed
driving a mechanical mole with sixteen jacks
two inches at a time through shifting silt,

and when air leaks and water follows
and you find yourself on shore in Weehawken,
wet and naked and miserable as a newborn –

the surfacing's not so sweet.
Try again: the thought rebounds.
And again: and it rebounds.

There's chatter of multiple universes.
There's talk of a rumor of a whisper
of a silence ten-times removed from the human voice.

Not unless you can build a bridge,
not unless you can take me there –
for every intimation, a civil engineer!

And once we've tied a bow around the infinite,
something pink and pretty in a bunny ear knot,
we'll see it's hardly bigger than a sonnet:

Your fixed *Infinito*, Leopardi, the one we return to,
not because it affirms your genius,
but because, for a little while, you sat on a hill

and surrendered to illusion.

Walking the Editor's Dog

He hates the rain, but loves to swim
and roll in mud, when walking him
he often sniffs through such morass
with such resolve that when he asks
with crooked head, What was the smell
that started this? I long to yell:
It's your own shit, it's your own piss,
there's nothing else of interest
to old black dogs with awkward gaits
and lingering pangs for former mates,
with tired paws, still wont to scratch
the itches only hands can reach,
who've seen a home or two and know
that strangers come, that owners go
and leave behind such baffling whiffs
one almost hopes … The Hudson shifts,
heavy, sways like wet cement,
and I check my throat for the scarf again
I left at home, where I keep no pet –
as sweet as Bozo tends to get
in the evenings, when he stretches out
to nap, though not on rug or couch
or pillow, or any padded lie,
but leaves and leaves of poetry.

JAMES GRABILL

However Many

However many names are written on doors,
however many sad melts of cathedrals
of ice, however spontaneous the blue is
in a person who refuses to consider the current
unknowns, whatever starlight tattoos in the summer
lull, in the half-future tombs where bones lie
badly, in the keep of a dozen million hooves
on the rock and furious slides on a fault,
the stabs of hunger off the tables, however likely
the cells are to re-establish readiness after disruption,
or dusk is liable to break in the wave of flux
or germinated shifts of double helix, resulting
in cultures of aversion to the immediate, however
many still-rumbling undercurrent heaves
hammer in a downpour, whoever may be walking
around, denying their own earthworm innards
or necessary number of mothers and fathers,
however developed the language seems,
however many compulsive reactions to the future
tense or relaxation catching fire earlier in the season,
in the hard-wired ounces of corn-forced yields,
whether swimming in the temporal instantaneous
grain or slow process of being conjoined with glowing
antler branches under Pacific shade, with mammalian
tipping points that cry out on the cutting edge
of 5 a.m., the hurricane eye which naturally selects,
muscling muds where emptiness cooks up
suddenly slow unseasonable stirring Bosch
open-arterial refinery vats, wheeling incomplete
acreage iron-bellied in muds, however
unthinkable the future appears to be looking.

A Chant: Converging in the Air

The swinging of cycles at the root of heat
and bearings on the ground, the coyote
circling back behind languages of the species,

the overpour arcing solid blue at beginnings
of contemplation within filtering membranous
bioswales of psyche, the ladling out of unfolding
spiral genome that settles down into cells,

the parallel chambers of cello, Bach crackling
with integrity in the evolution undergone
by a womb-walled fetus, the falling lift
that fills the simple rounding-off of apple,

conscious sense of mother in the collective
body of rain, the Bartók shadow thrown off
by flames of abstract winds, blue concentration
that rises to rooms buoyant over sealevel,

a chickadee in C-sharp threading her flight
in between stone going back to fresh anonymity,
her curve in the pull or draw of prismed sound.

Poetry Salzburg Pamphlet Series 7

Pnina Shinebourne
Radioactive
May 2013. 24 pp. ISBN 978-3-901993-38-1
£3.50 (+ 1.00 p&p), €4.50 (+ 1.00 p&p), US$6.00 (+ 1.50 p&p)

"Shinebourne tells the human story behind the discovery of radio-activity. She explores the interior thoughts, the intellectual conflicts, and the joys of scientific revelation. The style is clipped, heady, energised, and supple in its response to the hectic demands of the protago-nists, and the language is simple and immediate in the way it handles complex scientific ideas. Shinebourne captivates us by revealing the psychological pressures that give birth to the creative process and for this alone the pamphlet is a compelling read from start to end!"

Daljit Nagra

Collectors' Piece

After Éric Rohmer's film *La collectionneuse*

He saw her first in Rudolf's room
under him.
It was as if the figurine he stroked had made her moan.
Adrian shut the door after him.

She came south to where he holidayed
in Rudolf's sea retreat, and Daniel too.
She came in small hours from late parties
penetrating his sleep with drawn-out sex in the next room.
Her boy left at noon on his purring scooter
leaving her to lounge like a cat with the day before her
to wait for her new date – the one she'd fixed on the phone.
At night another cub rolled up the dusty drive
leaned on his open car whistling,
and when she was ready, drove her to the port where music played.

Adrian slept.
The co-co-rico of farm birds woke him.
He stepped down from the house for the close cove
as she came in smiling naughtily, naturally,
passed him and went up for day sleep.

Standing at the edge contemplating morning water
he envisaged her:
pretty
playful
passionate.

Then he dived.

July sky's clear in the early day,
sea stretches out to a dark promontory,
distant, tapering into whiteness.
Out deep's washed ultra marine,
blue-green shallows stippled
where the faint breeze ruffles.
Rocks – grey – stand out in the water,
hour-glass-fine sand's pale yellow,
grass, coarse, on the fading slope.
A trunk – half light, half dark – leans a little
and dark green ferns form a partial frame.
Slight shadows slant to the north and to the west
inclining the light of a Midi terrain,
a settled sea, quiescent as in Claude Lorrain.

DANIEL (at an open window): I'm on holiday. No effort – don't
want to make any at all.
ADRIAN (feet up on rustic sofa): Why don't you make a play for
Haydée?
DANIEL: Ah, no – and even if I wanted to I'd not succeed.
Anyway, I decided long ago not to run after any girl. It tires me
out. She's charming, yes, but that type doesn't interest me.
(He shrugs) She won't want me.
ADRIAN: Be serious, Daniel.
DANIEL: I am. Besides, I don't want to be part of her collection.
ADRIAN: The boys she's brought here aren't bad.
DANIEL: It's of no importance. I don't care whether a girl likes
me or not. I've come here for peace, not for complication. Just
reading in the shade of the tree is enough – and when I'm
rested, I'll go back to Paris, to my studio, and carry on with my
work. I've got a new project to start soon – a big free-standing
piece – this time for a company.
ADRIAN: Suit yourself. You don't need to take my advice.
(Daniel smiles, shakes his head, and picks up his book.)

It was early morning when Adrian came back from the port. No-one was around, though the birds were singing. The air smelt fresh as he went up the steps to the house. It was quiet inside, except when he mounted the stairs, which creaked. Passing her door, he saw the bedclothes ruffled; passing Daniel's door, he saw four legs entwined.

Sculpture

It's a tin painted in circles:
its base is crimson,
above, a thin circle of yellow;
rising, green merges with it,
next it blue.
One third's these rings of colour,
the rest's lemon to the lip
and painted lid.
Fixed vertically,
dark razor blades
puncture the sides
surrounding it.
It is hard to handle;
Rudolf does – and cuts his finger.
He thinks the tin is thought shut in,
the blades its protection.
Daniel perceiving he's keen
smiles cryptically.

In the morning Daniel sulked;
he would hide what had happened.
Adrian kept up a cutting irony
making it known he knew.
Haydée suffered. The men had hurt her.
Daniel was showing no warmth
and Adrian seemed piqued.
She would go back to her port boys,
swim with them by day, dance with them at night.
She was no collector as Adrian accused.
It was a definition she emphatically refused.

[178]

Collectors premeditate, and she did not.
They seek to complete sets, and she did not
though she sought completion.

At the port she was surprised to find Adrian kind,
that he brought her his jacket in the fresh night,
was gracious to her in the crowd,
behaved as an escort should.
With ease she forgave him his vexing,
acknowledged his praise of the red sky,
accepted his suggested walk in the glowing hills,
early bathe in his quiet cove.

She dived
and he with her.
They could see weed waving
shoals scatter
stones many-shaped in the shallows
deep azure above.
She saw his legs stretching
pushing the water in whirls
his arms stroking
his long hair waving like the weed
his mouth bubbling under the surface
lips seeming to smile in the distorting water.
With that she rose to breathe
in the blue, lie afloat
aface the canopy, to bathe in radiance.

She slept
her bed warm on sun-struck sand
sleep lapped by shore water
a humming coming closer passing over
sea to land where the birds call in the morning
they breathe on her
put wet lips to her skin
peck at her neck
– she woke
felt his breath at her neck

[179]

his fingers on her thigh
his body hard on her.
Touched, she rolled away
offhand, grabbed at sand
and flung it.
His eyes were offended.
She could see his head shaking out the beach,
his body bent, his fingers in his hair.
She turned to go,
saw Daniel on the slope,
ran to him and caught his hand.
He laughed, perhaps perfunctorily,
perhaps at Adrian,
she didn't care –
she'd let him laugh,
he'd had his chance at love.

Hi – I'm Stan.
American, yes.
In Nice, for a long time now – since I got divorced.
Do? I'm a collector of Chinese artifacts – mostly vases.
I'm here because it's where the money is – and the taste.
My business has gotten me a villa with a pool and a Mediterranean view
(that's my Rolls parked over there).
I like good food and fine wines.
I have women to stay sometimes – but not for long.
I prefer to be surrounded by my art objects – especially my vases –
they talk to me, but they don't talk back.
I'm both hedonist and ascetic, you know, and aesthete too
– not a misogynist, if that's what you're thinking.
Now there's this guy Adrian I've just bought a beauty from
(really special, tenth-century *Song* – rare).
I don't get him: he has a talent for finding things – and he doesn't sell
cheap –

but he lives like a student, staying in other people's places,
doesn't seem to own a thing.
And there's this cute babe, Haydée (cute name too),
he's staying with along the coast, and there's another guy

a sculptor or some such, turning out garbage from garbage.
A ménage à trois? I guess not.
He seems indifferent to her, even wants to palm her off on me.
I don't mind if he does, so long as he takes her back.
It's the bowed necks of vases I like to hold fast to and fondle.
– Nice talking to you. Enjoy your vacation. Ciao.

Objet d'art

It was fired a millennium ago in not-too-hot heats
standing whole today on based rectangle
not damaged by time, tempest or trade,
without break, crack or chip.
Under lustre its colours are still clear
– vital dyes from ancient times lasted in hard lights
deep réséda encompassing the vessel;
gamboge too in parts where green's not fixed.
From the foot, horse waves seem whipped by sea squalls
reaching up at bowed stem
bifurcating to petals or leaf of white at full width
till there's a shallow narrowing at the neck
where heads of paired elephants long gone from Cathay's plain
stand out like handles for the moving when drooping blooms are changed.

She'd spent the night at Stan's
swam in his cool pool
got further bronzed
and in the evening lounged on his lazy leather sofa.
Adrian sat opposite cross-legged while Stan mixed the drinks.
She told him Stan was sweet
but didn't say she'd shared his bed.
Adrian didn't ask, though he wanted to.
He'd not forgotten the sand in his face.
Stan came back with the drinks.
They chatted.
The drinks were strong.
Had he plied her when he was gone?
With his heavy-purse he'd not need to,

[181]

she'd easily add him to her collection.
"Stan, you're a perfect piece", Adrian says.
"And you, Adrian, are cracked – worthless."
"And Haydée?"
"Haydée's honey."
Stan reaches out at her.
She withdraws teasingly behind a pedestal table.
Stan follows pretending a chase.
There's the vase on the table at its centre.
She's behind it dodging, pretending evasion.
The table – touched – dances on two feet.
The vase joins in – first on four corners – then one
chasséing to terracotta – and shatters.
Her fingers are on the table to steady it, unready.
Adrian sees her pixie face in suspension.
Stan slaps it and wishes a pox on her.
Seeing the pieces, something dies in him,
bits of color without meaning, like a torn-up check.
All that's left to show once exquisite shape:
cracked trunk and broken neck.

Portrait

There's a pedestal table she's standing at
fingers pressed on polished wood
summer arms giving them weight ensuring her stamp.
The round of her shoulders meets her dress
a circle of bottle-green follows firm-sure bounds
a round of royal blue nestles in at a neat waist
green, again, converges on a tight-high bottom.
Upward pan to the face: Is it amused? Or might it be amazed?
There's a look not clear – of naughtiness, perhaps, or guilt?
Her mouth's held in – almost in shock –
but her cheeks are high and there's laughter in her eyes.
There's someone beyond me she's fixed on
whose response she hangs on in hesitation
before mirth might burst from her pert mouth
or those high cheeks fall and be rained on.

In Stan's marble bathroom Haydée cried,
settled in Adrian's arms
and – after stroking – kissed him succulently.
They would go home and make overdue love.
They'd be a couple now – at least until the summer's end.
So he drove her in the late-evening light
fast through hill villages
along rock-hewn roads
she squealing at hairpin bends
not looking at the drop
clinging to him firm at the wheel.
They came to a pass with red arrow pointing,
stopped to let a coming car get by.
"Haydée!"
It was convertible and the top was down.
"Haydée!"
There were young men in it – front and back –
one taking off his shirt.
"Where have you been, Haydée? We've missed you."
Now they were alongside.
"Haydée, why don't you come with us? There's a party at the port."
Adrian looked ahead at the rock face, his own mirroring it.
The girl got out.
To him she said, "I'm coming", though it might have been to them.
There was mirth and a round of double-kisses.
Then came a double-hooting from behind – someone impatient to pass.
Adrian's foot was on the pedal: the dial read – 35 – 50 – 60 …
His foot kept pressed down, though he'd not meant it.
Now he'd not stop, nor would he collect her.
He'd leave Haydée to her many mates
while he'd travel singly on the next express,
glance at the *Paris-Presse*
and, in the glass, reflect on his reflection,
on Daniel's dumb dance
on Stan's smashed *Song*,
most on Haydée, whose high-cheeked smile had so heated him
and seemingly cheated him.
Thus, heading north, he'd have his thoughts collected.

[183]

MICHAEL BLACKBURN is a lecturer at the University of Lincoln. His most recent collections are *Big on the Hawkesbury* (The Knives Forks and Spoons Press, 2010) and *Pocket Venus* (The Red Ceilings Press, 2011). He has been an editor on *Stand Magazine*, a Literature Development Worker, festival director, and Royal Literary Fund Fellow.

ELIZABETH BURNS' fourth collection of poetry is *Held* (Polygon, 2010). Her sequence of elegies, *The Shortest Days* (Galdragon Press, 2008), won the inaugural Michael Marks Award for Poetry Pamphlets. She teaches Creative Writing and lives in Lancaster in NW England.

HÉLÈNE CARDONA is the author of *Dreaming My Animal Selves* (Salmon, 2013), *The Astonished Universe* (Red Hen Press, 2006), and the forthcoming *Life in Suspension* (Tupelo Press). She attended the International University of Menéndez Pelayo, Spain and holds an MA in American Literature from the Sorbonne. Hélène translated for the NEA and the Canadian Embassy, and received fellowships from the Goethe-Institut and the Universidad Internacional de Andalucía.

VUYELWA CARLIN was born in South Africa in 1949 and brought up in Uganda. She has lived for many years in Shropshire. Collections to date: *Midas' Daughter* (1991), *How We Dream of the Dead* (1996), *Marble Sky* (2002), and *The Solitary* (2008; all Seren).

JOHN WEDGWOOD CLARKE trained as an actor at the Guildhall School of Music and Drama and has a DPhil in Modernist Poetics from the University of York. He also works as UK and Ireland editor for Arc Publications and teaches poetry freelance on the part-time creative degree at the University of Hull. His debut pamphlet *Sea Swim* was published by Valley Press in 2012. He grew up in St. Ives, Cornwall, and now lives in Scarborough.

HARRY CLIFTON, born in Dublin in 1952, won the Patrick Kavanagh Award in 1981. He returned to Ireland in 2004 and is currently Ireland Professor of Poetry. He has published five collections of poems, including *The Desert Route: Selected Poems 1973-88* (1992) and *Night Train through the Brenner* (1994), both from The Gallery Press, and *Secular Eden: Paris Notebooks 1994-2004* (Wake Forest UP, 2007) which won the Irish Times Poetry Now Award. His most recent collection *The Winter Sleep of Captain Lemass* was published by Wake Forest UP and Bloodaxe in 2013.

GAIL DENDY lives in Johannesburg. Her first collection, *Assault and the Moth*, was published by Harold Pinter's Greville Press in 1993. Her seventh collection was entitled *Closer Than That* (Dye Hard Press, 2011).

ROGER DESY taught Literature and Creative Writing and later edited technical manuals. His poems have appeared in *Blue Unicorn*, *Cider Press Review*, *Kenyon Review*, *Mid-American Review*, *The Pinch*, and *Poet Lore*.

CRAIG DOBSON ran a retail business for twenty years until he decided to commit fully to writing poetry. He has completed a Creative Writing MA at Bath Spa University in 2012. His poems have appeared in *The Frogmore Papers*, *The Interpreter's House*, and *The North*.

KEVIN DUCEY's short stories, essays, and poems have appeared in *AGNI*, *Crab Orchard Review*, *Crazyhorse*, *Exquisite Corpse*, *Notre Dame Review*, and *The Pinch*. His first book of poems, *Rhinoceros*, won the American Poetry Review's Honickman Award and was published by APR in partnership with Copper Canyon Press in 2004.

PAUL DURCAN was born in Dublin in 1944. His first book, *Endsville* (New Writers' Press, 1967), has been followed by more than twenty others, including *The Berlin Wall Café* (a Poetry Book Society Choice, 1985), *Daddy, Daddy* (winner of the Whitbread Award for Poetry, 1990; both Blackstaff), *A Snail in My Prime: New and Selected Poems* (1993), *Cries of an Irish Caveman: New Poems* (2001), *The Art of Life* (2004; all Harvill Press), *The Laughter of Mothers* (2007), and *Praise in Which I Live* and *Move and Have My Being* (2012; both Harvill Secker). In 2009 Random House published a selection of his work from the previous forty years in one volume, *Life Is a Dream*. In 2001 Paul Durcan received a Cholmondeley Award. He was the Ireland Professor of Poetry 2004-2007. In 2009 he was conferred with an honorary degree by Trinity College, Dublin. He is a member of Aosdána.

SCOTT ELDER lived as a busker and mime in Paris, London, and Portugal before spending twelve years in retreat in a Buddhist hermitage in Auvergne. He now resides in France with his wife and three young children. His poems have been published by *Plein Page Editeur* and *Poetry Cornwall* and will be appearing in the forthcoming issues of *The Antigonish Review*, *Nimrod International Journal*, and *Orbis*.

BLAIR EWING. Former child TV actor, lifeguard, golf-course drone, congressional intern, political pollster, and assistant brain at The United States Institute of Peace. Published 2 books of poems, both by Argonne House Press in Washington, DC: *Chainsaw Teddybear* (1999) & *And to the Republic* (2002). Also produced 2 CD anthologies of Baltimore poets. Poems recently published in *The Federal Poet*, *Gargoyle*, *Heeltap*, *Jones Av*, *LitSpeak*, and *Taj Mahal Review*.

ANNIE FINCH is the author of more than twenty books of poetry, plays, translation, literary essays, textbooks, and anthologies, most recently *A*

Poet's Craft: A Comprehensive Guide to Making and Sharing Your Poetry (U of Michigan P, 2012), *Villanelles* (Random House, 2012), and *Spells: New and Selected Poems* (Wesleyan UP, 2013). She is the winner of the Sarasvati Award for her poetry and the Robert Fitzgerald Award for her work in versification.

JOHN TEMPLE FINNIGAN was born in 1953 and raised in South Shields, on the North East Coast of England. He moved to London in 1977 and since then he has been published in magazines like *The London Magazine*, *Orbis*, and *Sentinel Poetry Quarterly*.

KATE FOX was born in Bradford in 1975 and qualified as a radio journalist before becoming a full time poet, performer, and creative facilitator in 2006. In 2012 her one-woman Edinburgh show *Kate Fox News* toured the UK. Her work has appeared in *Aesthetica*, *Anon*, *Magma*, and *Under the Radar*. Pamphlets include *Why I* (Zebra Press, 2005), *We Are Not Stone* (Ek Zuban, 2006), and *Kate Fox News* (New Writing North, 2010). *Fox Populi* (Smokestack Books, 2013) is her first collection. She is about to begin a PhD researching solo stand-up performance. She lives in North Yorkshire.

WILLIAM GILSON is an American living permanently in England. Recent publications include a novella, "At the Dark End of the Street", in *New England Review*. He is co-author of *Carved in Stone: The Artistry of Early New England Gravestones* (Wesleyan UP, 2012).

JAMES GRABILL's poems have appeared in numerous periodicals, most recently in *The Chariton Review*, *The Common Review*, *The Harvard Review*, *New York Quarterly*, *The Oxonian Review*, *Shenandoah*, and *Stand*. His books of poems include *An Indigo Scent after the Rain* (2003) and *Poem Rising Out of the Earth and Standing Up in Someone* (1994; both Lynx House). He lives in Oregon, where he has taught writing and literature.

VONA GROARKE was born in the Irish Midlands in 1964. Her collections published by The Gallery Press (and by Wake Forest UP in the United States) include *Shale* (1994), *Other People's Houses* (1999), *Flight* (2002), shortlisted for the Forward Prize (UK) in 2002 and winner of the Michael Hartnett Award in 2003, *Juniper Street* (2006), and *Spindrift* (2009), a Poetry Book Society Recommendation. Her next collection, *X*, is due in 2014. Her poems have recently appeared in *The Guardian*, *Kenyon Review*, *Poetry Review*, *The Times*, and *Yale Review*. She now lives in Manchester where she teaches in the Centre for New Writing at the University of Manchester.

DANIEL HARDISTY was born in Bradford in 1978. He studied English and Creative Writing at the University of East Anglia. His poems have appeared in *New Welsh Review*, *Poetry Ireland Review*, *Poetry London*, *The Rialto*, *The SHop*, *Smiths Knoll*, *The Spectator*, and elsewhere.

BARBARA HARDY was born in Swansea and educated at Swansea and University College London. She is an Emeritus Professor at Birkbeck, University of London, and Hon. Professor of English at University of Swansea. She is a Fellow of the Royal Society of Literature and the British Academy. She specializes in the work of Jane Austen, Charlotte Brontë, Dickens, George Eliot, Shakespeare, Thackeray, and Dylan Thomas. Poetry collections: *London Lovers* (Peter Owen, 1996, Sagittarius Prize), *Severn Bridge: New and Selected Poems* (Shoestring Press, 2001), *The Yellow Carpet* (Shoestring Press, 2006), and *Dante's Ghost* (Paekakariki Press, 2013).

MARC HARSHMAN has published one full-length collection, *Green Silver and Silent* (Bottom Dog Press, 2012), four chapbooks, and eleven children's books, including *The Storm* (Dutton Juvenile, 1995), a Smithsonian Notable Book. His poems have appeared in magazines like *5 AM*, *The Georgia Review*, *The Progressive*, and *Shenandoah*. Harshman was appointed the new poet laureate of West Virginia in 2012.

MATT HAW is a poet, critic, librettist, and gardener. He was the recipient of an Eric Gregory Award in 2013 for *Saint-Paul-de-Mausole*, a book-length sequence after the life and work of Van Gogh. He currently lives in Andalusia.

WENDY HOLBOROW's poems have appeared in magazines such as *Agenda*, *Envoi*, and *Poetry Ireland Review*. She has recently completed a poetry mentorship with Literature Wales and is starting an MA in Creative Writing at Swansea University in September.

SARAH HYMAS lives on Morecambe Bay. Her writing has appeared in single collections, magazines, anthologies, multimedia exhibits, dance videos, lyrics, theatre programmes, pyrotechnical theatre shows, and as an improvised opera. Her collection, *Host*, was published by Waterloo Press in 2010.

JERZY JARNIEWICZ is a poet, translator, and literary critic. He is the author of nine critical books and eleven volumes of verse. The latest are *Oranżada* ("Orangeade"; 2005), *Makijaż* ("Make-up"; 2009), and *Na dzień dzisiejszy i na chwilę obecną* ("Today and at this moment in time"; 2012). He is a professor of English Literature at the University of Łódź and has for many years been associated with *Literatura na świecie* ("Literature and the World"), Poland's most important journal of translation.

CAROLYN JESS-COOKE's poetry has been published in *Magma*, *Poetry London*, *Poetry Review*, *The SHOp*, *The Stinging Fly*, and others. Her international bestselling prose has been translated into 22 languages.

ANTONY JOHAE has a PhD in Comparative Literature (Essex, 1980) and has taught in England, Germany, Ghana, Tunisia, and Kuwait. Since 2009 he has lived in Lebanon and is now writing freelance.

DEBASISH LAHIRI teaches English Literature at Lal Baba College, under the University of Calcutta. His first collection *First Will and Testament* was published by Writers Workshop, Kolkata, in 2012. He is also a regular contributor to *The Statesman*, Kolkata.

ANDREW LATIMER has recently graduated from the University of Glasgow, with First Class Honours in English Literature. He will be studying for an MA in English at Oxford, St. John's with a particular interest in Ezra Pound's use of the typewriter.

ROBERT LEACH was born in Huddersfield, Yorkshire, and educated at Pembroke College, Cambridge University. He is a theatre practitioner and historian. He has a PhD from Cambridge University and was Reader in Drama and Theatre Arts at the University of Birmingham before becoming Senior Lecturer in English and European Literature at Edinburgh University. He has had three collections of poetry published: *Boy and Baggage* (2001), *Sour Cream* (2006), and *After the Storm* (2011; all Dionysia Press). His poetic epic, *The Journey to Mount Kailash*, was published by Indigo Dreams in 2010.

MARK LEECH has published two chapbooks, *London Water* (Flarestack, 2008) and *Chang'an Poems* (Original Plus, 2012). His poems and translations have appeared in a wide range of magazines including *Agenda*, *Magma*, *MPT*, *The Reader*, *Tears in the Fence*, and *The Wolf*.

DAN MACISAAC's poetry has appeared in many journals, including *Agenda*, *Arc*, *Cirque*, *The New Quarterly*, and *South Carolina Review*. His translations of the poetry of Lorca, Ovid, and others have appeared in magazines like *The Antigonish Review*, *The Malahat Review*, *Prism*, and *Willow Springs*. He lives on Vancouver Island on the west coast of Canada.

JULIE MACLEAN is originally from Bristol, UK, and now lives on the Surf Coast, Australia. Her debut collection of poetry, *When I Saw Jimi*, was published in June 2013 by Indigo Dreams.

DAVID MALCOLM is a professor of English at the University of Gdańsk. He co-edited and co-translated *Dreams of Fire: 100 Polish Poems, 1970-1989* (Poetry Salzburg, 2004). His translations from Polish and German have appeared in many countries.

DAVID MOHAN is based in Dublin, Ireland, and received a PhD in English Literature from Trinity College. He is published in or has work forthcoming in *The Chattahoochee Review*, *Contrary*, *elimae*, *New World Writing*, *Opium*, *Southword*, and *Stirring*. In 2012 he won the Cafe Writers' International Poetry Competition.

EILÉAN NÍ CHUILLEANÁIN was born 1942 in Cork and educated in Cork and Oxford. Poet and Emeritus Professor of English, Trinity College, Dublin, where she has taught since 1966 – she still teaches on Translation and Comparative Literature courses after her retirement in 2011. Co-founder with Macdara Woods, Leland Bardwell, and Pearse Hutchinson of the literary magazine *Cyphers*. Her *Selected Poems* was published by The Gallery Press and Faber in 2008. Her latest book, *The Sun-Fish* (The Gallery Press, 2009; Wake Forest UP, 2010), was awarded the 2010 International Griffin Poetry Prize. She is married to the poet Macdara Woods, and they have one son, Niall, a musician. They live in Dublin and in Umbria.

CATH NICHOLS has a PhD in Creative Writing from Lancaster University and is an associate lecturer at Leeds University. Her publications are two pamphlets, *Distance* (erbacce press, 2012) and *Tales of Boy Nancy* (Driftwood, 2005), and a collection, *My Glamorous Assistant* (Headland, 2007).

JAMES B. NICOLA was published in periodicals including *Atlanta Review*, *Lyric*, *Nimrod*, and *Texas Review*. A Yale graduate and stage director by profession, his book *Playing the Audience* (Applause, 2002) won a Choice Award. Also a composer, lyricist, and playwright, his children's musical *Chimes: A Christmas Vaudeville* premiered in Fairbanks, Alaska.

JAMES NORCLIFFE lives near Christchurch, New Zealand. He has published eight collections of poetry, the most recent are *Packing a Bag for Mars* (Clerestory Press, 2012) and *Shadow Play* (Proverse, 2012). His work has appeared in *Ariel*, *The Baltimore Review*, *Landfall*, *London Magazine*, *The Malahat Review*, *Orbis*, *The Rialto*, and *Stand*. He was the 2000 Robert Burns (Writing) Fellow at the University of Otago (Dunedin, NZ). He has twice won the NZ Poetry Society's International Prize.

JANE NORTH is a teacher and poet living in Cremona, Italy. Her poems have been published in *California Quarterly*, *The Interpreter's House*, *Poesia*, *Poetry Cornwall*, *Poetry New Zealand*, *Private Photo Review*, and *South Africa Literary Journal*.

CAITRÍONA O'REILLY is an Irish poet and critic. She has published two collections of poetry with Bloodaxe Books and has written for *The Guardian*, *The Irish Times*, *Poetry Review*, and *The Times Literary Supplement*. She served on the editorial board of *Metre Magazine* and as editor of *Poetry Ireland Review* from 2008 until 2011.

FRANK OSEN's first book, *Virtue, Big as Sin*, was awarded the 2012 Able Muse Book Prize by poet Mary Jo Salter and published by that press in 2013. His poetry has appeared or is forthcoming in *The American Arts Quarterly*, *The Dark Horse*, and on Ted Kooser's *American Life in Poetry*. He has won the Best American Poetry Poem Contest #2. He lives in Pasadena, California, where he works at the Huntington Library.

WILLIAM OXLEY was born in Manchester, UK. His most recent books are *ISCA: Exeter Moments* (Ember Press, 2013) and translations (with Parvin Loloi) from *The Divan of Hafez* (Acumen Publications, 2013). Forthcoming in 2014 is his *Collected and New Poems* from Rockingham Press. Poetry Salzburg published *The Romantic Imagination: A William Oxley Casebook* in 2005. He is a former member of the General Council of the Poetry Society. Co-founder of the Torbay Poetry Festival, he received the Torbay ArtsBase Award for Literature in 2008.

THOMAS PIEKARSKI is a former editor of the *California State Poetry Quarterly*. His poetry has appeared in journals like *Clockhouse Review*, *Cream City Review*, *Kestrel*, *Main Street Rag*, *New Plains Review*, *Nimrod*, *Penny Ante Feud*, *Poetry Quarterly*, *Portland Review*, and *Scarlet Literary Magazine*. He has published a travel guide, *Best Choices in Northern California*, and a book of poems, *Time Lines* (Nimbus Press, 2010). He lives in Marina, California.

COLIN PINK lives in London. He writes plays and poetry. His poems have appeared in various magazines, such as *Coffeehouse*, *Pen-Pusher*, *The SHOp*, *Trespass*, and *Urthona*. His plays have been performed in the UK, USA and in translation in Germany.

TODD PORTNOWITZ's most recent work has appeared in *Antioch Review*, *Birmingham Poetry Review*, *CalibanOnline*, and *The Journal of Italian Translation*. Todd received an MA in Italian Literature in 2012, and works as a freelance editor and translator in New York City.

FRANK C. PRAEGER is a former research biologist who lives on the Keewenaw Peninsula which juts out of the northwest end of the Upper Peninsula of Michigan into Lake Superior. He has had poems published in *Bolts of Silk*, *Dead Snakes*, *Full of Crow*, *Ink Sweat & Tears*, *London Grip*, *The Recusant*, and *The Rusty Nail*.

MICHAEL PRIOR is a graduate student at the University of Toronto. His poems have appeared in *The Antigonish Review*, *Branch Magazine*, *Carousel*, *CV2*, *ditch*, *filling Station*, *FreeFall*, *Grain*, and *Qwerty*.

J. STEPHEN RHODES has an MFA from the University of Southern Maine and a PhD from Emory University. His poems have appeared in *The International Poetry Review*, *Shenandoah*, *The SHOp*, and *Tar River Poetry*, among others. His poetry collection, *The Time I Didn't Know What to Do Next*, was published in 2008 by Wind Publications.

PETER RILEY was born into an environment of working people in the Manchester area in 1940 and now lives in retirement in Hebden Bridge, having previously lived in Cambridge for 28 years. He has been a teacher, bookseller, and a few other things and is the author of some fifteen books of poetry, and two of prose concerning travel and music. His most recent book is *The Glacial Stairway* (Carcanet, 2011). He contributes reviews of new poetry to the website *The Fortnightly Review*.

MARK ROBINSON lives in Eaglescliffe near Stockton-on-Tees. His New & Selected Poems *How I Learned to Sing* was published by Smokestack Books in 2013. He is the founder of Thinking Practice, through which he works with arts organisations in a variety of ways. He was the founder of *Scratch* magazine and press, which he ran from 1989 to 1997.

STEWART SANDERSON is a first year PhD candidate in Scottish Literature at Glasgow University. His poems have appeared in *Cyphers*, *Gutter*, *Irish Pages*, *Magma*, *Poetry Review*, and *Poetry Wales*.

IAN SEED is editor of Shadowtrain books and webzine. His publications include *Sleeping with the Ice Cream Vendor* (The Knives Forks and Spoons Press, 2012), *Threadbare Fables* (Like This Press, 2012), *Shifting Registers* (Shearsman, 2011), *Amore mio* (Flax, 2010), and *Anonymous Intruder* (Shearsman, 2009).

HILDA SHEEHAN is a mother of 5 children and has been a psychiatric nurse and Montessori teacher. She is editor of *Domestic Cherry* magazine and also works for Swindon Artswords (Literature Development) and the Swindon Festival of Poetry. Her first collection, *The Night My Sister Went to Hollywood*, was published by Cultured Llama Press in 2013.

IAN C. SMITH's work has appeared in *The Best Australian Poetry*, *Chiron Review*, *Island*, *Quarterly Literary Review Singapore*, *Southerly*, and *Westerly*. His latest book is *Here Where I Work* (Ginninderra Press, Adelaide, 2012). He lives in the Gippsland Lakes area of Victoria, Australia.

KATHRINE SOWERBY is a Glasgow based poet with a background in fine art. She has been published in journals like *Fractured West*, *Gutter*, and *Northwords Now*.

SHELBY STEPHENSON's *Family Matters: Homage to July, the Slave Girl* (Bellday Books, 2008) won the 2008 Bellday Poetry Prize. From 1979 to 2010 Shelby Stephenson served as editor of *Pembroke Magazine*.

COLIN SUTHERILL lives near Leominster. His collection, *Einstein's Bumblebee* (Blackwater), appeared in 1997. He is also published by *Ambit*, *Envoi*, *Erbacce*, *Fire*, *The Rialto*, and *Stride*.

WALLY SWIST's books include *Velocity* (2013), *Winding Paths Worn through Grass* (2012; both Virtual Artists Collective), and *Huang Po and the Dimensions of Love* (Southern Illinois UP, 2012). His *Selected Poems* is forthcoming from FutureCycle Press in 2014. His poems have most recently appeared in *Blueline*, *The Cape Rock*, *Connecticut Review*, *Crab Orchard Review*, *Empirical Magazine*, *Miriam's* and *Wild River Review*.

FIONA SZE-LORRAIN is the author of two books of poetry, *My Funeral Gondola* (Manoa Books/El Leon Literary Arts, 2013) and *Water the Moon* (Marick, 2010), as well as many books of translation of Chinese, French, and American contemporary poets. She lives in France where she works as an editor and *zheng* harpist.

CASSANDRA QUINN THOMAS is a freelance writer whose poems appeared in *Pen Women Magazine* and *Riverrun*. She holds an MAT in Southwest Studies from Colorado College.

JOHN SIBLEY WILLIAMS is the author of *Controlled Hallucinations* (FutureCycle Press, 2013) and six poetry chapbooks. He serves as editor of *The Inflectionist Review*, co-director of the Walt Whitman 150 project, and Marketing Director of Inkwater Press. A few previous publishing credits include: *Bryant Literary Review*, *The Chaffin Journal*, *Cider Press Review*, *Cream City Review*, *The Evansville Review*, *Inkwell*, *RHINO*, and *Third Coast*. He lives in Portland, Oregon, USA.

GEOFFREY WINCH's poetry has been published in journals including *Envoi*, *Fire*, *Iota*, *Sarasvati*, *South*, and *South Bank Poetry*. His tanka have appeared in journals such as *Blithe Spirit*, *Modern English Tanka*, and *Ribbons*. His third collection, *Letting the Road-Dust Settle* (Indigo Dreams, 2010), coincided with his retirement as a highway engineer.

RICHARD WOTTON is a translator who lives in Berlin. His poems have recently been published in *The Frogmore Papers*, *Orbis*, and *Upstairs at Duroc*.

SIEGFRIED ZADEMACK, born 1952 in Bremen, is a German Surrealist Artist. He has worked as a freelance artist since 1980. His work has been exhibited internationally. His surrealistic visionary paintings are often ironical, deal with mythology and metaphysics, and probe into the depths of the human soul.